KITES, BIRDS & STUFF.

by P.D.STEMP.

MILES

AIRCRAFT

Kites, Birds & Stuff
MILES Aircraft.
by P.D.Stemp.
2010 Lulu Author.
All rights reserved.

ISBN 978-1-4457-7645-3

MILES AIRCRAFT Ltd.
F.G.Miles and friend Cecil Pashley interest in aircraft started in the early 1920's.
They got together to share their aspirations and over a period of years gathered a collection of aircraft (with the financial help of F.G's father), which they employed mainly in their joyriding business ?.
F.G.Miles later married to Blossom Miles and both joined the firm of Phillips & Powis Aircraft (Reading) Ltd., which was later formed into Phillips & Powis Aircraft Ltd., during 1935.
During October 1943 the name of the manufacturers Phillips & Powis Aircraft Ltd., was changed to :-
MILES AIRCRAFT Ltd. - formed at Woodley, Reading.
In November 1947, went into liquidation and the aircraft interest were taken over by Handley Page.

MILES AIRCRAFT (N.I.) of Newtownards, Northern Ireland.
Formed by C.O.Powis, production ceased during January 1948.

F. G. MILES Ltd.
Formed in 1951 at Redhill, Surrey and transferred to Shoreham, Sussex. in 1952.
Acquired by British Executive & General Aviation during February 1961 - **BEAGLE-MILES Ltd.**
In April 1962 formed into - **BEAGLE AIRCRAFT Ltd.**

MILES CONSTRUCTIONAL METHODS

1. Fitting the plywood skin to a Master fuselage. 2. A Master centre-section spar is boxed in. 3. A one-piece wing leading-edge is fitted. 4. Framework and plywood skin of a fin unit. 5. A rudder unit in its jig. 6. Plywood skin being applied to a main plane.

MILES MARTLET

Previous to the Martlet F.G.Miles had built a Gnat biplane to the final assembly stage, this was during 1925, but he never flew it.

During 1928, F.G. & G. Miles designed and built with the assistance of D.L.Brown and H.Hall, the Martlet. Of a wooden construction using spruce, ash, plywood and fabric covering, using some Avro spares which had been purchased earlier.

A single seat advanced trainer and sporting aircraft, also known as the - **'HORNET BABY' & 'SOUTHERN MARTLET'**.

The prototype - G-AAII - was powered by 75 h.p. A.B.C.Hornet four cylinder radial engine.
Six of the type were built priced at £ 600 = each, numbers :-
200 / G-AAII / EI-ABG, later re-engined with 80 h.p. Armstrong Siddeley Genet II five cylinder radial engine.
201 / G-AAVD, powered by 80 h.p. A.S.Genet II engine and flew for the first time on the 24-3-1930.
202 / G-AAYX,   "   " 105 h.p. A.S. Genet Major five cylinder radial engine.
203 / G-AAYZ,   "   " 120 h.p. Gipsy II four cylinder in line engine, later re-engined with a 100 h.p. De Havilland Gipsy 1 engine and the aircraft was scrapped during 1937.
204 / G-ABBN, powered by 80 h.p. Armstrong Siddeley Genet II engine and scrapped during 1935.
205 / G-ABIF,   "   as 204.

Performance
Maximum speed. 112 m.p.h.
Cruising   "   95 m.p.h.
Landing   "   40 m.p.h.
Climb rate. 1,100 ft./min.
Range. 285 miles.
Duration. 3 hrs.
Fuel capacity. 15 gallons.

Dimensions
Span. 25 ft. - Length. 20 ft. 3 ins.
Height. 7 ft. 6 ins. - Wing area. 180 sq. ft.

Weights
Empty. 630 lbs. - Loaded. 1,040 lbs.

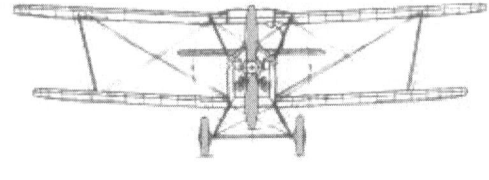
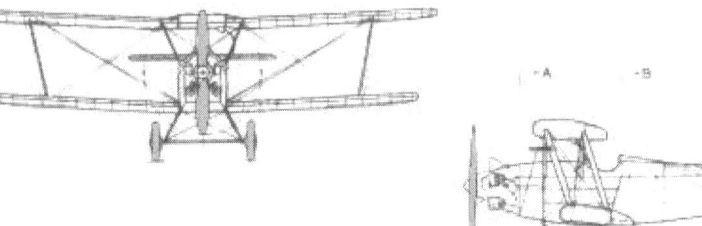

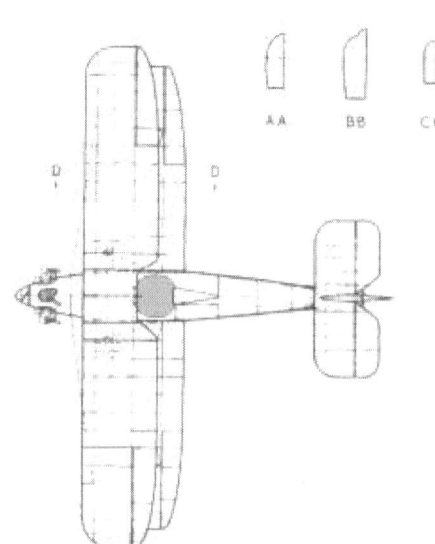

MILES METAL MARTLET

A single seat advanced training and sporting aircraft.
Of a metal construction, fitted with detachable wood and fabric fairings.
The folding wings were of wood and fabric covered, as was the tail unit.
One only - G-AAJW, the registration number should have been - G-ABJW - which flew for the first time during 1930 and was scrapped during November 1932.
Powered by 105 h.p Cirrus Hermes four cylinder in line air cooled engine.
A second of the type was started upon - G-ABMM - but never finished.

Performance
Maximum speed. 130 m.p.h.
Cruising   "   115 m.p.h.
Landing   "   40 m.p.h.
Climb rate. 1,400 ft.
Service ceiling. 20,000 ft.
Range. 400 miles.
Duration. 3 hrs. 30 mins.

Dimensions
Span. 23 ft. 6 ins. - 9 ft. 4 ins.
Length. 20 ft. 6 ins. - Height. 8 ft. 3 ins.
Wing area. 156 sq. ft.

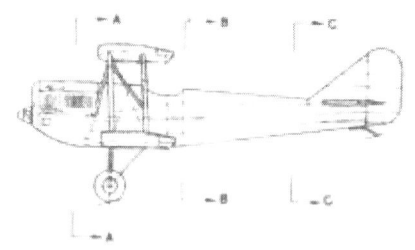

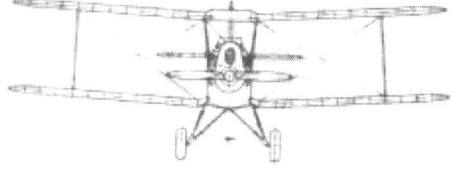

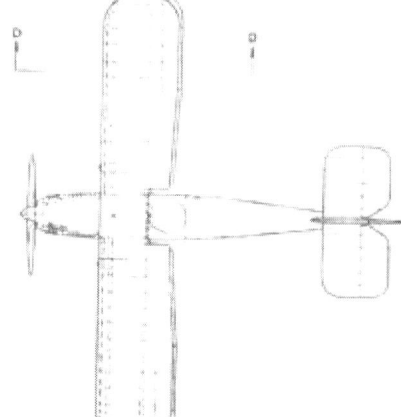

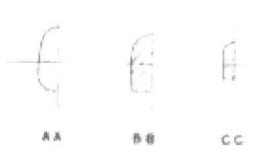

MILES M.1 SATYR

A small single seat sporting bi-plane aircraft, designed by F.G.Miles and built by George Parnall & Co., during 1931.
Of a wooden construction and fabric covered.
Powered by 75 h.p. Pobjoy R seven cylinder radial engine.
One only - G-ABVG - flew for the first time during August 1932, crashed and written off in 1936.

Performance
Maximum speed. 125 m.p.h.
Cruising   "   110 m.p.h.
Landing   "   40 m.p.h.
Climb rate. 1,400 ft./min.

Dimensions
Span. 21 ft. upper - 18 ft. lower.
Length. 17 ft. 8 ins. - Height. 5 ft. 9 ins.
Wing area. 117 sq. ft.

Weights
Empty. 594 lbs. - Loaded. 900 lbs.

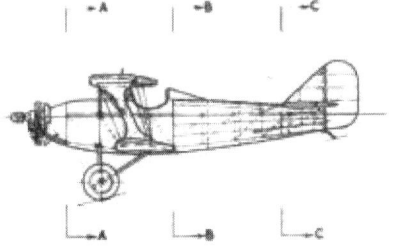

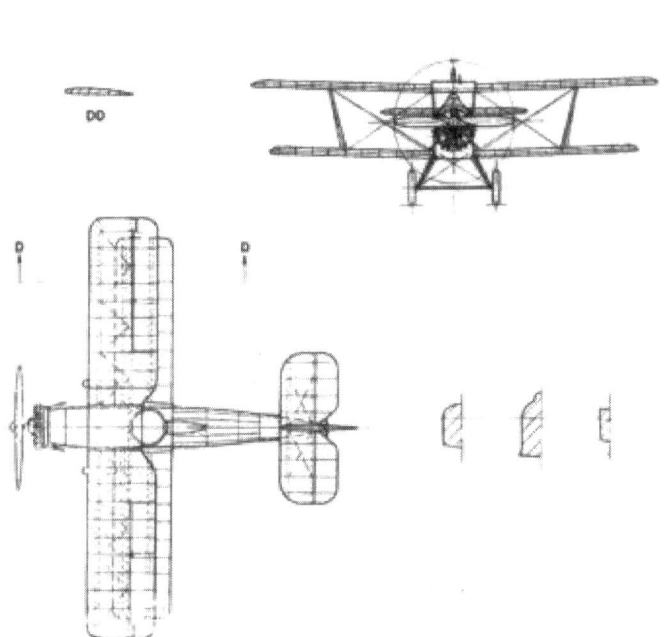

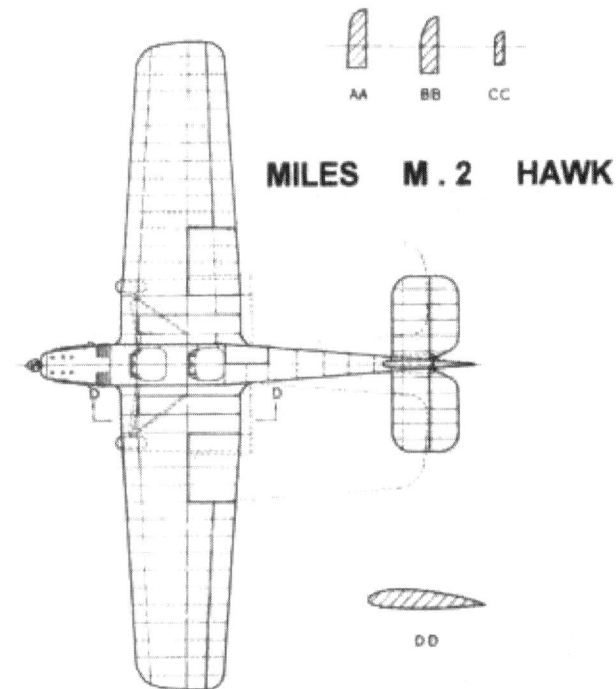

MILES M.2 HAWK

MILES M.2 HAWK

A light two seat touring and training monoplane aircraft, built by Phillips and Powis Aircraft (Reading) Ltd.
The fuselage is constructed of a Spruce framework, plywood covered.
The wings are of Spruce spars and ribs, plywood covered and could fold.
The tail unit is of a wooden framework and fabric covered, all for the cost of > £ 395 =, later £ 495 =.
The prototype - G-ACGH - which flew for the first time on the 29-3-1933.
Powered by 95 h.p. A.D.C.Cirrus IIIA four cylinder in line air cooled engine.
The first production Hawk - G-ACHJ - appeared on the 8-7-1933, as a single seater competing in the Kings Cup Race.
The second production type - G-ACHK - appeared two weeks later.
Nos. 1 / G-ACGH - G-ACHJ - G-ACHK - G-ACHL - G-ACHZ - G-ACIZ - G-ACJC - G-ACJD -
G-ACJY - G-ACKI - G-ACKX / PK-SAL - G-ACLA - G-ACLB - G-ACMH - G-ACMM -
G-ACMX / EI-ABQ - G-ACNW - 24 / G-ACNX - G-ACOC - G-ACOP - G-ACPW - G-ACRB -
G-ACRT - G-ACSD - G-ACSL - G-ACTI - G-ACTN - G-ACTO / CH-380 / AW 152 - G-ACUD -
G-ACVN - G-ACVO - G-ACVP - G-ACYA - G-ACZD - G-ACZG - G-ACZI - G-ACZW - G-ADBK -
G-ADDM - G-ADGI / AW 150 - G-ADGR - G-ADVR / YR-ITR, not delivered.

M. II A - Fitted with an enclosed cabin and powered by 120 h.p. De Havilland Gipsy III engine.
Nos. 14 / G-ACLI.
M. II B - A single seat long range version, powered by 120 h.p. A.D.C.Cirrus Hermes IV engine.
Nos. 12 / G-ACKW / VT-AES.
M. II C - Powered by 120 h.p. De Havilland Gipsy III engine.
Nos. 19 / G-ACOB / F-AMZW.
M. II D - A three seater, powered by 95 h.p. A.D.C.Cirrus IIIA engine.
The types were also fitted with other engines, such as :- De Havilland Gipsy Six and Major engines, Hermes II B's also Cirrus R engines.
Nos. 20 / G-ACPC - 30 / G-ACPD - 32 / G-ACSX - 35 / G-ACSC - 108 / G-ACVR.

A total of 55 Hawk aircraft were built, mainly with constructors numbers from 1 to 92.

Performance
Maximum speed. 115 m.p.h. - 140 m.p.h. A - 160 m.p.h. B - 114 m.p.h. D.
Cruising   "   100 m.p.h. - 125 m.p.h. A - 140 m.p.h. B - 98 m.p.h. D.
Landing   "   42 m.p.h.
Take off run. 150 / 180 ft.
Climb rate. 860 ft./min.
Service ceiling. 16,000 ft. - 18,000 ft. D.
Range. 450 miles II / D - 1,000 miles. A - 2,000 miles B.
Fuel capacity. 22 1/2 gallons.

Dimensions
Span. 33 ft. - 13 ft. 10 ins. folded - 35 ft. D.
Length. 24 ft. - Height. 6 ft. 8 ins.
Wing area. 169 sq. ft.

Weights
Empty. 1,104 lbs. - 1,045 lbs. D.
Loaded. 1,800 lbs. - 2,200 lbs. B.

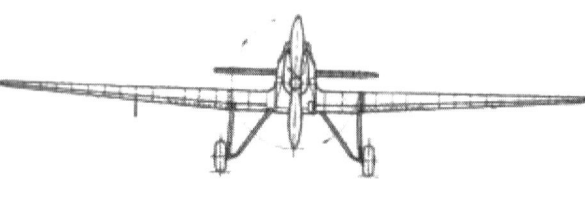

MILES M.2 HAWK MAJOR

A development of the Hawk, initially as a two seat high performance light monoplane aircraft.
The construction is of a Spruce framework and plywood covering for the fuselage.
The wings have Spruce spars and plywood ribs, which are plywood covered.
The tail unit is of a wooden framework and fabric covered.
Fitted with metal engine mountings and a cantilever trousered undercarriage.
M. II F - The prototype - 36 / G-ACTD - Powered by 120 h.p. De Havilland Gipsy Major III four cylinder in line air cooled engine.
The following sixteen production types were powered by 130 h.p. De Havilland Gipsy Major engines.
Fitted with a single strut faired undercarriage and the price for this new fully equipped aircraft is :- £ 750 =
Nos. 109 / G-ACVM - 110 / G-ACWV - 111 / G-ACWW - 112 / G-ACWX - 113 / G-ACWY / NF 748 -
114 / G-ACXL - 115 / G-ACXM / VT-AGX - 116 / G-ACXN / VP-KBL - 117 / G-ACYW / EC-ZZA -
118 / G-ACXT / DG 577 / 4020M - 119 / G-ACXU / ZK-ADJ - 120 / G-ACYB / HB-OAS -
121 / G-ACYO / NF 752 - 134 / G-ADAC - 147 / G-ADCI / ZK-AFM - 166 / G-ADGL - 169 / G-ADGA.
M. II E - **The Gipsy Six Hawk** - The prototype - 43 / G-ACTE - a special single seat racing variant.
Powered by 200 h.p. De Havilland Gipsy Six engine and flew for the first time during June 1934.
Later modified with a sliding hood and renamed - **Hawk Speed Six.**
Hawk Speed Six - Referred usually to those types powered by the De Havilland six cylinder engines, of which there were three :- M IIE - M IIL - M IIU.
There were many variants of this type, including :-
M. II F - A two seat touring and training type, powered by 130 h.p. De Havilland Gipsy Major engine.
Modifications to the engine cowling, fuselage front end and single strut cantilever trousered undercarriage.
Nos. 217 / G-ADVF - 224 / G-ADWU - 228 / G-ADWV - 126 ? / SU-AAP / HK 863
M. II G - A three seat cabin version - 120 / G-ADCV / HB-OAS.
M. II H - Powered by 130 h.p. De Havilland Gipsy Major engine and fitted with a trailing edge flap.
Nos. G-ACYX / F-BCEX - G-ACYZ - G-ACZI - 122 / G-ACZJ / VT-AIR / LV 768 - G-ADAB - G-ADAS -
G-ADAW - G-ADBG - G-ADBT - G-ADCF - G-ADCJ - G-ADCU - G-ADCW - G-ADCY - G-ADDC -
G-ADDU - G-ADEN - G-ADFC - G-ADGD - G-ADGE - 166 / G-ADGL - G-ADHF - G-ADIG -
G-ADIT / X 5126 / 3017M - G-ADLA - G-ADLB - G-ADMW / DG 590 - G-ADZU - G-AEEZ - G-AEFA -
124 / G-AEFS - G-AEGE / HL 538 - G-AEGP / DP 851 / 3016M - G-AEGR - G-AEKJ -
G-AENS / DP 848 - 328 / G-AENT - G-AEOX - G-AFKL.
144 / ? / VT-AGH
M. II L - 160 / G-ADGP - Powered by 200 h.p. De Havilland Gipsy Six IF engine.
Later modified with a bubble hood.
M. II M - 159 / G-ADCV - Powered by 130 h.p. De Havilland Gipsy Major engine.
A three seater, the pilot in an open cockpit and the two passengers behind in an enclosed glazed cabin.
M. II P - Powered by 130 h.p. De Havilland Gipsy Major engine.
Nos. 190 / G-ADDK / BD 180 - 220 / G-ADLO / ZK-AFL - 251 / VP-KBT / ZK-AFJ.
M. II R - Powered by 130 h.p. De Havilland Gipsy Major engine, later re-engined with a Menasco Pirate C 4 engine.
Nos. 194 / G-ADLH - 211 / G-ADLN / DG 664 - **The Hawk Major de-Luxe.**
Later modified with a Menasco Pirate C IV engine
M. II S - 194 / G-ADLH - Long range version built during 1935.
Powered by 150 h.p. Blackburn Cirrus Major engine.
M. II T - Long range single seat types - Nos. 203 / G-ADNJ - 222 / G-ADNK.
Powered by Blackburn Cirrus Major engines.

Picture above shows :- Miles M.2 L Hawk Major.

MILES M.2 HAWK MAJOR

M. II U - Powered by 200 h.p. De Havilland Gipsy Six R high compression engine.
195 / G-ADOD.
M. II W - Hawk trainer, powered by 130 h.p. De Havilland Gipsy Major engine.
Fitted with dual controls, larger cockpit openings, vacuum operated flaps and blind flying equipment.
Nos. 215 / G-ADWT / NF 750 / CF-NXT - 217 / G-ADVF - 224 / G-ADWU - 228 / G-ADWV.
M. II X - Hawk trainer, of which twenty five were built, during 1936, with horn balanced rudders.
Powered by 130 h.p. De Havilland Gipsy Major engine.
Nos. 235 / G-ADYZ - 241 / G-ADZA / DG 665 - 242 / G-ADZB - 246 / G-AEAW - 249 / G-ADZC -
254 / G-ADZE - 260 / G-AEAX / DG 666 - 270 / G-AEAZ - 271 / G-AEEL.
M. II Y - A batch of thirteen aircraft, similar to the M IIX, powered by 130 h.p. De Havilland Gipsy Major engine.
Nos. 237 / G-AEHR - 245 / G-AEHS - 253 / G-ADZD - 258 / G-AEHP - 261 / G-AEAY -
265 / G-AEHT - 292 / G-AEHU - 293 / G-AEHV - 294 / G-AEHW - 295 / G-AEHX - 296 / G-AEHY -
297 / G-AEHZ - 302 / ZK-AEQ.
The type were also produced under licence in Spain and India.

Performance
Maximum speed. 150 m.p.h. - 185 m.p.h. E / U - 192.83 m.p.h. L.
Cruising   "   135 m.p.h. - 160 m.p.h. E / L / U .
Landing   "   42 m.p.h. - Landing run. 270 ft. - Take-off run. 240 ft.
Climb rate. 1,000 ft./min. F / H / M - 1,450 ft./min. E / L / U - 1,300 ft./min. W / X / Y.
    "   "   to 10,000 ft. 9 mins. 15 secs.
Service ceiling. 20,000 ft. F / H / M - 18,000 ft. W / X / Y.
Range. 740 miles. - 560 miles. F / H / M - 400 miles W / X / Y.
Duration. 5 hrs. 30 mins.
Fuel capacity. 33 gallons.

Dimensions
Span. 33 ft. - 34 ft. P / R / W / X / Y - 13 ft. 10 ins. folded.
Length. 24 ft. - Height. 6 ft. 8 ins.
Wing area. 169 sq. ft. - 174 sq. ft. P / R - 176 sq. ft. W / X / Y.

Weights
Empty. 1,355 lbs. E / L / U - 1,150 lbs. F / H / M - 1,210 lbs. W / X / Y.
Loaded. 1,800 lbs. F / H / M - 1,900 lbs. E / L / U / P / R - 1,720 lbs. W / X / Y.
Petrol & Oil. 270 lbs. - Payload. 300 lbs.
Pilot. 160 lbs. - Disposable. 730 lbs.

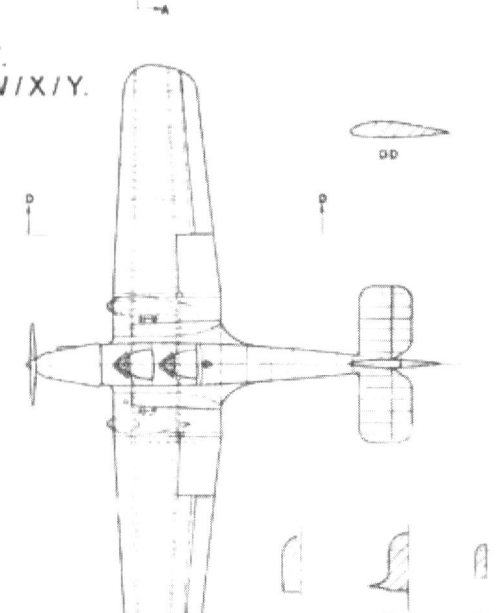

MILES M.3 FALCON

A three or four seat cabin monoplane, structurally similar to the Hawk Major.
Of a wooden construction with Spruce members and plywood covering.
The prototype - 102 / U-3 / G-ACTM - flew for the first time on the 12-10-1934, as a three seat cabin monoplane.
On the production machines the windscreen was sloped forward from the top inwards to the base and the wings could also fold.

M. III A - Falcon Major - The production types, with dual controls, hydraulically operated split flaps, a wider fuselage to seat four and a modified cabin top.
The first production type - G-ADBF - flew for the first time during January 1935.
Powered by 130 h.p. De Havilland Gipsy Major engine.
Nos. 131 / G-ADBF / I-ZENA temp./ HB-USU - 140 / G-ADBI - 157 / G-ADER / F-AQER -
163 / G-ADHC / I-ZENA - 181 / G-ADHH / VQ-PAO - 189 / G-ADHI / X 9300 -
193 / G-ADHG / VH-AAT - 196 / G-ADFH / HM 496 - 202 / G-ADIU - 206 / G-ADLI -
209 / G-ADZR / VH-AAS - 216 / U-20 / G-AEEG / SE-AFN - 226 / G-AETN -
229 / G-AEFB / X 9301 - 234 / G-AENG.

M. III B - Falcon Six - As a three seater, the prototype - G-ADLC - flew for the first time on the 27-7-1935.
Powered by 200 h.p. De Havilland Gipsy Six inverted air cooled in line engine.
Nos. 213 / G-ADLC - 231 / G-ADLS - 233 / OE-DBB / G-AFAY - 247 / ZK-AEI - 248 / G-AEKK / W 9373 -
255 / G-ADTD - 256 / D-EGYV / G-AFBF / AV 973 - 259 / G-AEDL - 262 / G-ADZL -
269 / G-AEAO / PH-EAO.

M. III C - One only - 231 / G-ADLS - A dual controlled four seater.
M. III D - A strengthened variant :- Nos. 266 / G-AEAG / VH-ABT - 280 / G-AECC / DG 576.
M. III E - Powered by a 200 h.p. De Havilland Gipsy Six engine :-
Nos. 289 / G-AFCP - ? R 4071 / G-AGZX / OO-FLY.

'Gillette Falcon' - L 9075 - used as an experimental wing research aircraft, to assist in the development of the M. 52.
Production ceased during 1936, after a total of 36 aircraft were produced and some were still in service with the R.A.F. after the Second World War.

Performance
Maximum speed. 148 m.p.h. proto. - 145 m.p.h. A - 180 m.p.h. B.
Cruising   "   130 m.p.h. proto. - 125 m.p.h. A - 160 m.p.h. B.
Landing   "   40 m.p.h.
Climb rate. 750 ft./min. proto. / A - 1,000 ft./min. B.
    "   " to 5,000 ft. 4 mins. 55 secs. B.
    "   " " 10,000 ft. 11 mins. 34 secs. B.
Service ceiling. 15,000 ft.
Range. 615 miles A. - 560 miles B.
Fuel capacity. 32 gallons.

Weights
Empty. 1,270 lbs. proto. - 1,300 lbs. A - 1,550 lbs. B.
Loaded. 2,000 lbs. proto. - 2,200 lbs. A - 2,350 lbs. B.

Dimensions
Span. 35 ft.
Length. 25 ft.
Height. 6 ft. 6 ins.
Wing area. 174 sq. ft.

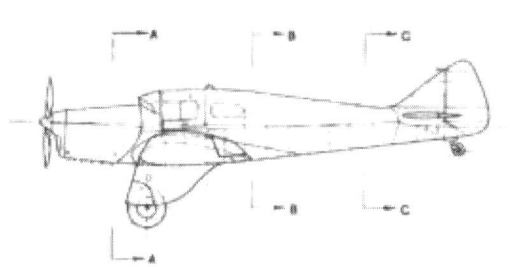

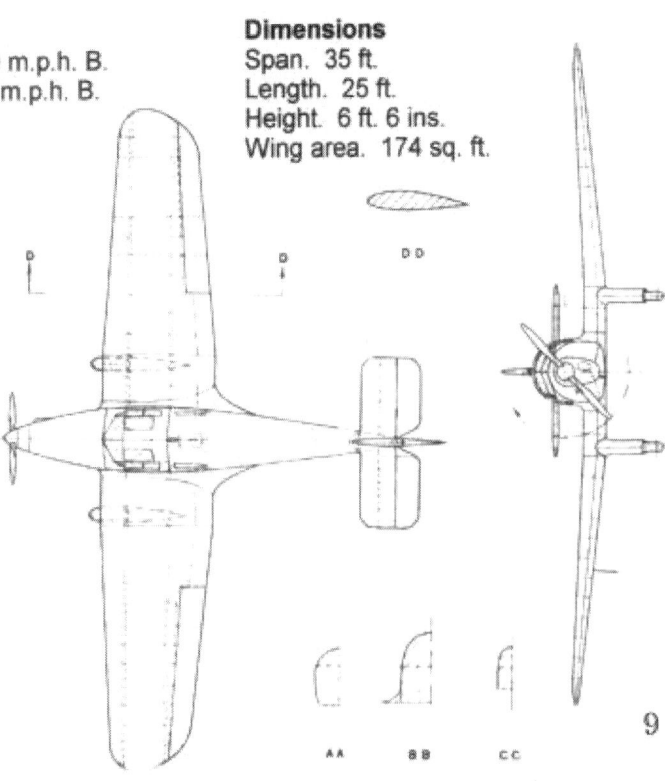

MILES M.4 MERLIN

A five seat touring and light commercial cabin monoplane.
Of an all wooden construction, with plywood and fabric covering.
The prototype - 151 / U 8 / G-ADFE - which flew for the first time on the 11-5-1935.
Powered by 200 h.p. De Havilland Gipsy Six inverted in line air cooled engine.
Four of the type were built.

Performance
Maximum speed. 155 m.p.h.
Cruising   "   140 m.p.h.
Landing   "   50 m.p.h.
Climb rate. 900 ft./min.
Service ceiling. 18,000 ft.

Dimensions
Span. 37 ft. - Length. 25 ft. 10 ins.
Height. 9 ft. 7 ins. - Wing area. 196 sq. ft.

Weights
Empty. 1,700 lbs. - Loaded. 3,050 lbs.

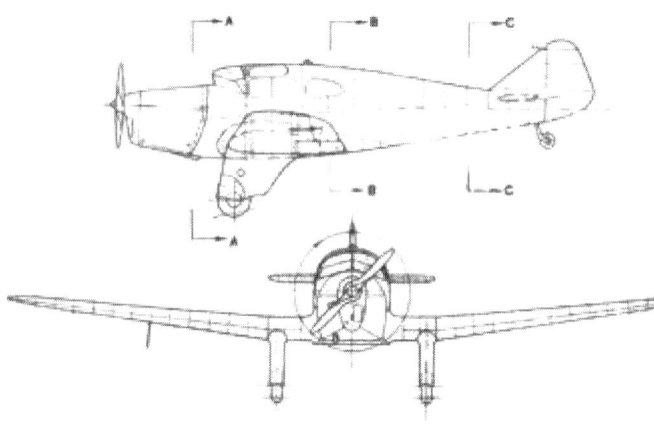

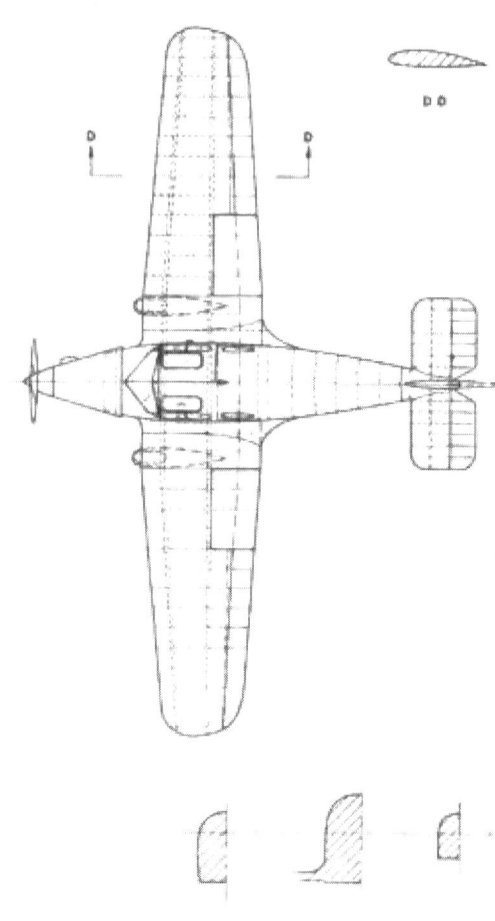

MILES M.5 SPARROWHAWK

A variant of the Hawk, the prototype - 239 / G-ADNL - a single seat racing monoplane, built during 1935.
Of an all wooden construction, with plywood and fabric covering.
Powered by 140 h.p. De Havilland Gipsy Major high compression four cylinder inverted in line air cooled engine.
The aircraft was also fitted with long range fuel tanks and flew for the first time on the 20-8-1935.
(See also :- Miles Sparrowjet - F.G.M.77 / 1006).
M. V A - Nos. 264 / G-ADWW / NC 191M - 275 / G-AELT / ZS-ANO - 273 / G-AFGA
The last of the type was built in June 1936 and was used for experimental purposes (high lift flap research) - 276 / U 3 / U-0223 / later G-AGDL.
Originally powered by 130 h.p. De Havilland Gipsy Major I engine and later by 145 h.p. De Havilland Gipsy Major II engine.

Performance
Maximum speed. 178 m.p.h. h/c.
Cruising   "   160 m.p.h. h/c.
Landing   "   42 m.p.h.
Range. 415 miles.

Dimensions
Span. 28 ft. - Length. 23 ft. 6 ins.
Height. 5 ft. 7 ins. - Wing area. 138 sq. ft.

Weights
Empty. 1,080 lbs. - Loaded. 1,750 lbs.

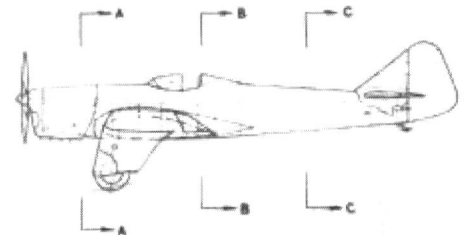
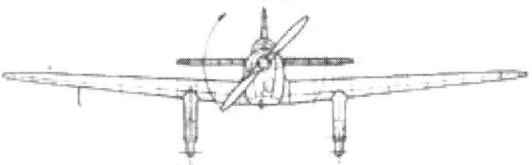

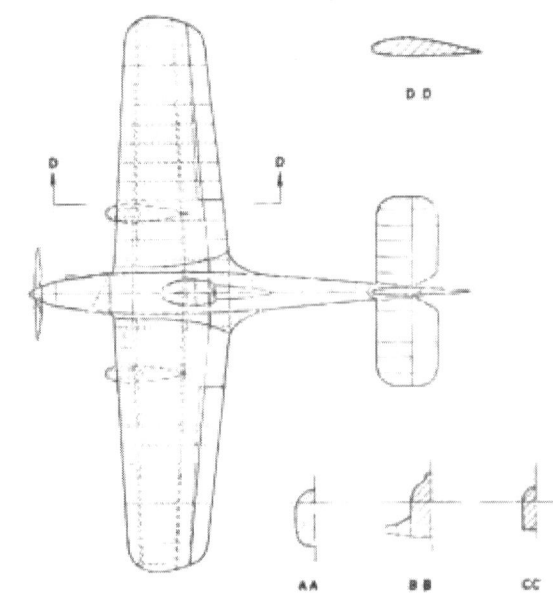

MILES M.6 HAWCON

A two seat experimental thick wing research aircraft.
Of a wooden construction, with plywood and fabric covering.
One only - K 5925 - which flew for the first time on the 29-11-1935.
Powered by 200 h.p. De Havilland Gipsy Six cylinder inverted in line air cooled engine.
Four sets of wings for the aircraft were built, with various root thickness to chord ratio -
From 15 % - 20 % - 25 % to 30 % - and as it proved there was only a difference of only 5 m.p.h. between all of the wings.

Performance
Maximum speed. 178 m.p.h. 15 % - 181 m.p.h. 20 % - 176 m.p.h. 25 % - 180 m.p.h. 30 %.

Dimensions
Span. 33 ft. - 39 ft. 5 ins. 30 %.
Length. 25 ft. - Height. 6 ft. 6 ins.
Wing area. 161 sq. ft.

Weights
Empty. 1,550 lbs. - Loaded. 2,400 lbs.

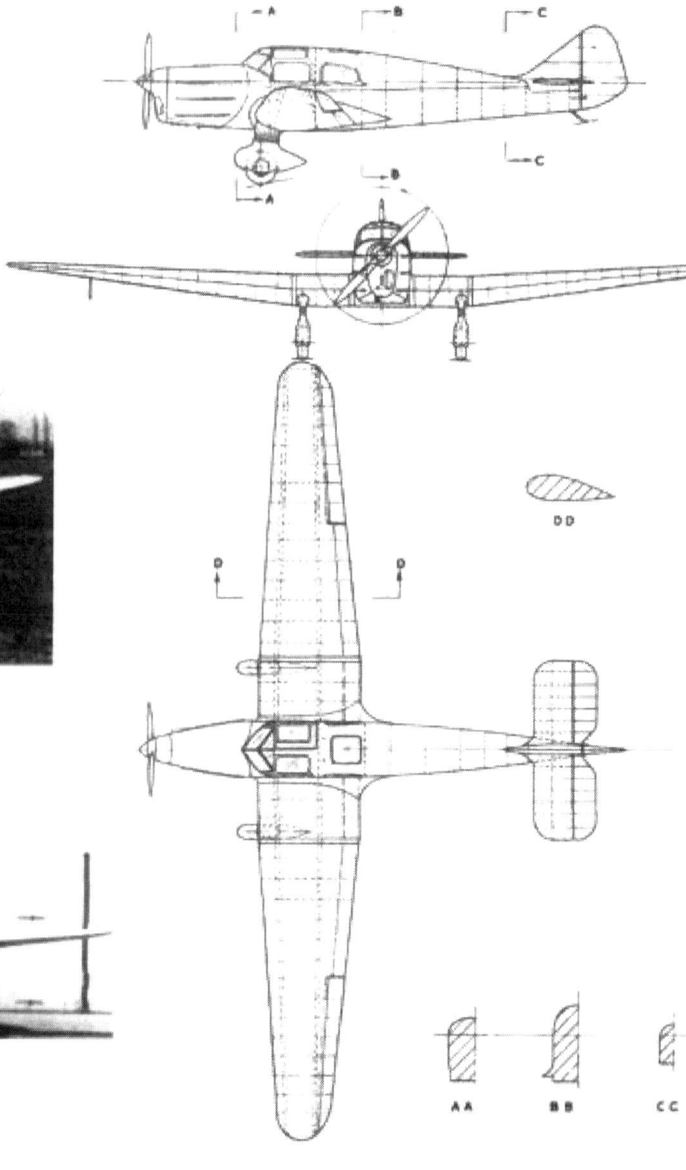

MILES M.7 NIGHTHAWK

Spec. 24 / 36.

A development of the Miles Falcon, originally as a private venture.
As a three seat light cabin monoplane aircraft, for communications duties.
As a four seater for training purposes, navigation, instrument / night flying, radio instruction and fitted with dual controls.
The prototype - No. 263 / G-ADXA - flew for the first time on the 18-12-1935.
Powered by a 200 h.p. De Havilland Gipsy Six engine.
Also produced were - Nos. 282 / G-AEBP - 283 / G-AEHN - 284 / G-AEHO.
M. VII A - Rebuilt in 1944, using a Nighthawk fuselage and the wings of the second Mohawk.
Powered by 205 h.p. De Havilland Gipsy Six II engine, with a variable pitch propeller.
One only - No. 286 / U 5 / U-0225 / G-AGWT / VP-KMM.

Performance
Maximum speed. 175 m.p.h. - 170 m.p.h. A.
Cruising   "   155 m.p.h. - 150 m.p.h. A.

Dimensions
Span. 35 ft. - Length. 25 ft.
Wing area. 181 sq. ft.

Weights
Empty. 1,650 lbs.
Loaded. 2,400 lbs. - 2,650 lbs. A.

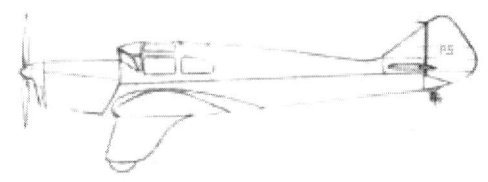

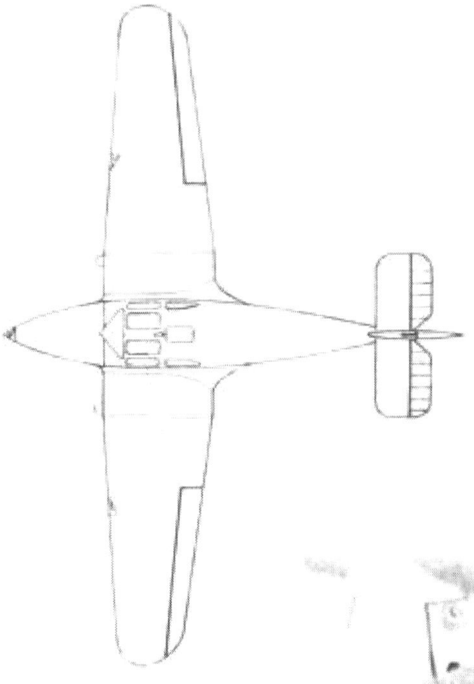

MILES M.8 PEREGRINE

The first twin engined aircraft produced by Miles.
A light transport aircraft, with a crew of two and accommodation for six to eight passengers.
Of an all wooden construction, with plywood and fabric covering.
Fitted with retractable undercarriage and dual controls.
A cabin of 12 ft. long x 4 ft. 6 ins. wide x 5 ft. high, with a volume of 218 cubic ft.
Only two aircraft were built - 300 / U 9 / G-AEDE - flew for the first time on the 12-9-1936
Powered by two 205 h.p. De Havilland Gipsy Queen II six cylinder engines, with variable pitch propellers.
The other - 485 / L 6346 - ordered by the Royal Aircraft Establishment, to be used as a flying laboratory.
Powered by two 290 h.p. Menasco Buccaneer B6S six cylinder engines and was one of the first Miles aircraft
to use duralumin sheet, fitted on its tail unit.

Performance
Maximum speed. 182 m.p.h.
Cruising   "   165 m.p.h.
Landing   "   55 m.p.h.
Climb rate. 960 ft./min. D.H.
   "   " 1,070 ft./min. Menasco.
Service ceiling. 23,000 ft.
   "   "   on one. 5,000 ft.
Fuel capacity. 80 gallons.
Oil   "   6   "

Dimensions
Span. 46 ft. - Length. 32 ft.
Height. 9 ft. 6 ins. - Wing area. 300 sq. ft.

Weights
Empty. 3,350 lbs. - Loaded. 5,500 lbs.

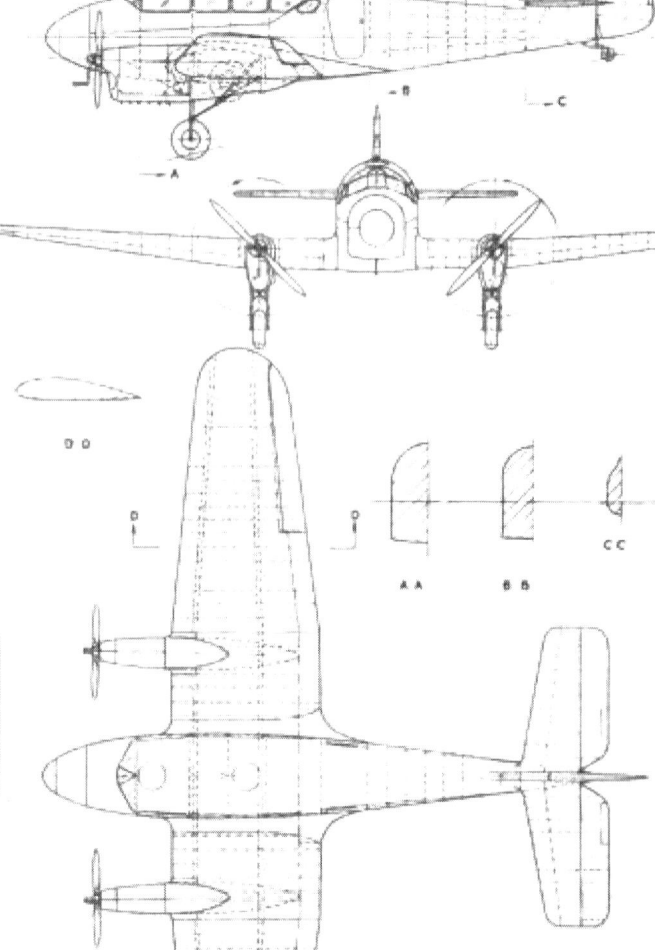

MILES M.9 KESTREL

A private venture, designed by F.G.Miles and built by Phillips & Powis Aircraft Ltd. at Woodley.
A two seat high speed advanced training aircraft, dual controlled and basically the Miles Master prototype.
Of a wooden construction, plywood and fabric covered.
One only - 330 / G-AEOC - flew for the first time during 3-6-1937 and was scrapped a year later.
Powered by 745 h.p. Rolls-Royce Kestrel XVI twelve cylinder water cooled Vee engine.
The aircraft could have been armed with a Browning machine in the Starboard wing, a camera could also be fitted in the Port wing.
It could also be fitted with racks under the wings to carry eight practice bombs.

Performance
Maximum speed. 296 m.p.h.
Cruising   "   254 m.p.h.
Landing   "   60 m.p.h.

Dimensions
Span. 39 ft. - Length. 29 ft. 6 ins.
Height. 9 ft. 5 ins. - Wing area. 235 sq. ft.

Weights
Empty. 4,159 lbs. - Loaded. 5,337 lbs.

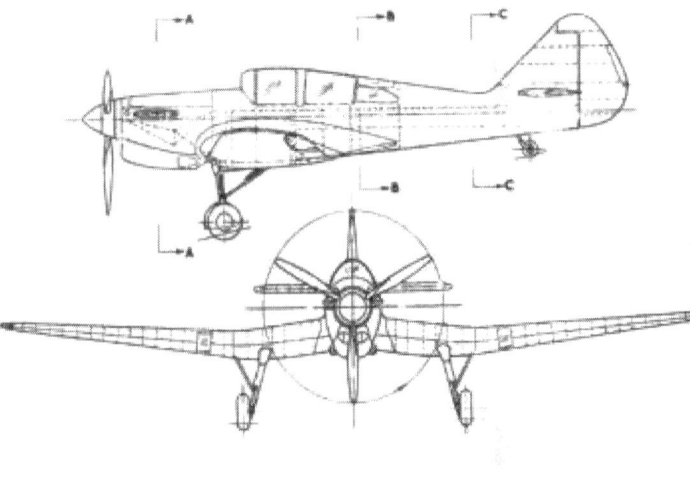

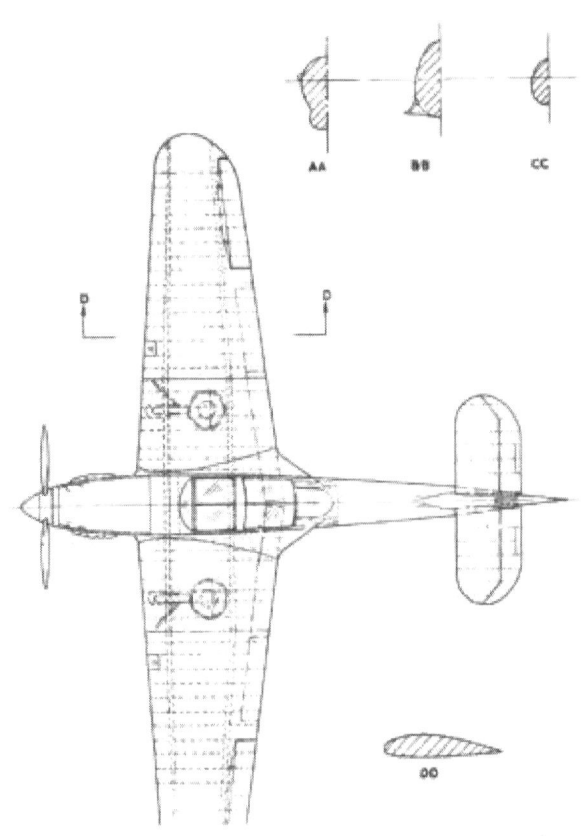

MILES MASTER M.9A MASTER I - M.19 MASTER II - M.24 MASTER FIGHTER - M.27 MASTER III

Manufactured by Phillips and Powis Aircraft Ltd., Woodley Aerodrome, Reading.
Originally a private venture designed to - *Spec. T. 6 / 36* - and known as the Kestrel, which flew for the first time on the 3-6-1937.
A two seat advanced training aircraft, with dual controls.
The aircraft is of a wooden construction, with plywood and fabric covering.
Powered by 745 h.p. Rolls-Royce Kestrel XVI engine, this the first prototype attained a speed of 295 m.p.h. at 16,500 ft.
The second prototype, known as the Master - N 3300 - appeared late in 1938 and was used as an experimental type, scrapped during 1943.

Mk. I - *Spec. 16 / 38.* - A two seat advanced training aircraft.
Of a similar construction as the M 9 Kestrel, but with a modified canopy, which was introduced during 1940 and strengthened rear fuselage.
Powered by 715 h.p. Rolls-Royce Kestrel XXX twelve cylinder water cooled Vee de-rated engine.
Armed with one fixed forward firing 0.303 Browning machine gun in the starboard wing, a camera in the Port wing and racks under the centre section for eight practice bombs.
Blind flying equipment, hood and instrument panel were provided in the front cockpit.
The first production Master I was - N 7408 - which flew for the first time on the 31-3-1939.
Deliveries of the type started during May 1939, a total of 900 were produced and the type were out of service by 1946.
Nos. 1111 / N 7408 to 1610 / N 9017 - T 8268 to T 8885.
Mk. I A - Fitted with a modified canopy, which was introduced during 1940.
M. 19 - Mk. II - The prototype - N 7422 - which flew in November 1939.
The production types were powered by 870 h.p. Bristol Mercury XX nine cylinder air cooled radial engine.
The instructor sat in the rear cockpit on a seat that could be raised and as it did so a flip up cockpit section operated.
A total of 1,799 were produced and later many of these were used as towing aircraft - **GT. Mk. II.**
The type remained in service until 1949.
Nos. N 7447 - T 8886, modified.
A production batch of 99 aircraft manufactured at Woodley :-
Nos. T 8887 to T 8923 - T 8948 to T 8967 - T 8996 to T 9037.
A second production batch of 525 aircraft manufactured at Woodley :-
Nos. AZ 104 to AZ 143 - AZ 156 to AZ 185 - AZ 202 to AZ 226 - AZ 245 to AZ 289 - AZ 306 to AZ 340 - AZ 359 to AZ 383 - AZ 408 to AZ 457 - AZ 470 to AZ 504 - AZ 519 to AZ 563 - AZ 582 to AZ 621 - AZ 638 to AZ 672 - AZ 693 to AZ 742 - AZ 773 to AZ 817 - AZ 832 to AZ 856.
Many of the batch were shipped to South Africa and AZ 672 was transferred to the U.S.A.A.F.
A third production batch of 500 aircraft manufactured at Woodley :-
Nos. DK 800 to DK 843 - DK 856 to DK 894 - DK 909 to DK 957 - DK 963 to DK 994 - DL 111 to DL 155 - DL 169 to DL 204 - DL 216 to DL 256 - DL 271 to DL 309 - DL 324 to DL 373 - DL 395 to DL 435 - DL 448 to DL 493 - DL 509 to DL 546.
DK 891, to Portugal - DL 131 to DL 151, to South Africa - DL 251 / 252 / 271 / 272 / 275 / 276 / 278 / 280, to Egypt - DL 302 to DL 309 plus DL 324 / 325 / 459, were converted to Glider Tug types.
A production batch of 86 aircraft manufactured at Swindon :- Nos. W 9004 to W 9039 - W 9050 to W 9099.
A second production batch of 212 aircraft manufactured at Swindon :-
Nos. DL 794 to DL 803 - DL 821 to DL 866 - DL 878 to DL 909 - DL 935 to DL 983 - DM 108 to DM 140 - DM 155 to DM 196.
DL 863 / 891 / 902 / 937 / 940 & DM 113 / 174, to Turkey - DL 976 to DL 979, DL 983 & DM 166 / 167 / 168 / 170 / 173 / 179 / 180, to Egypt.

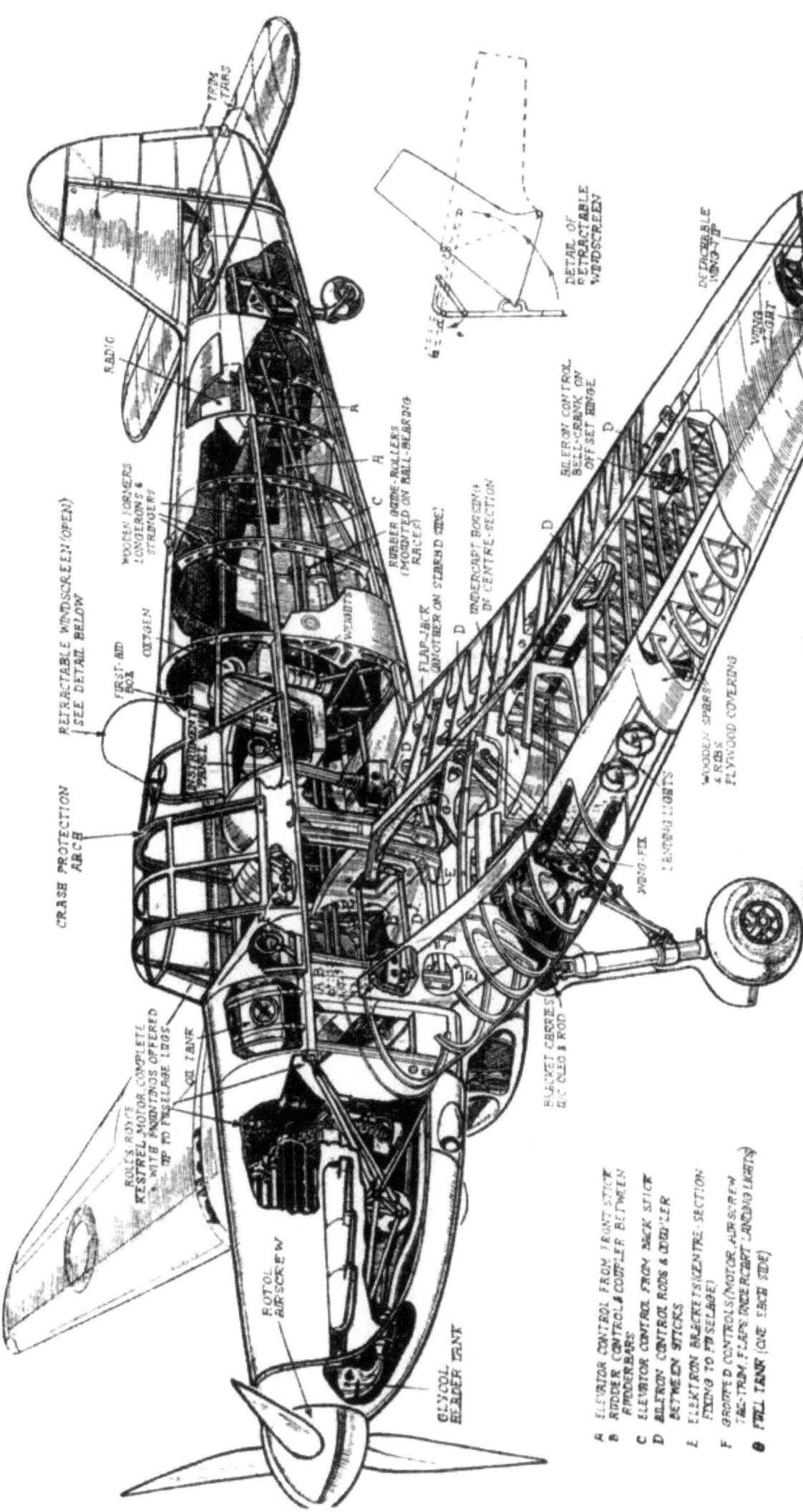

Miles Master M.27 Mk.III - W 8825

MILES MASTER

A production order for 300 aircraft, of which only 200 were built :- Nos. DM 200 to DM 245 - DM 259 to DM 295 - DM 312 to DM 361 - DM 374 to DM 407 - DM 423 to DM 454.
DM 434 Glider Tug - DM 442 / G-AIZN - DM 227 / 232 / 233 / 234 / 235, to Egypt - DM 231 / 276 / 335 / 346 / 351 / 376 / 454, to Turkey.
A fourth production batch of 125 aircraft manufactured at Woodley :-
Nos. EM 258 to EM 304 - EM 317 to EM 355 - EM 371 to EM 409.
EM 381 / 385 / 405, to Turkey - EM 300 / G-AIZM.

M. 24 - Master Fighter - Twenty five single seat fighter variants were built, these aircraft were armed with six 0.303 machine guns.

M. 27 - Mk. III - The last version, powered by the 825 h.p. Pratt and Whitney Twin Wasp Junior fourteen cylinder radial engine.
The prototype - N 7994 - flew during 1940.
Provision for night flying training was also provided in the front cockpit, plus two way radio and oxygen.
Production started with - W 8437 - and after a total of 602, production ceased in 1942.
The type remained in service until 1946.
A production batch of 414 aircraft manufactured at Swindon :-
Nos. W 8437 to W 8486 - W 8500 to W 8539 - W 8560 to W 8599 - W 8620 to W 8659 - W 8690 to W 8739 - W 8760 to W 8799 - W 8815 to W 8864 - W 8880 to W 8909 - W 8925 to W 8974 - W 8980 to W 9003.
A second production batch of 188 aircraft manufactured at Swindon :-
Nos. DL 552 to DL 585 - DL 599 to DL 648 - DL 666 to DL 713 - DL 725 to DL 753 - DL 767 to DL 793.
DL 670 / G-AGEK, to Irish Air Corps.

Performance
Maximum speed at sea level. 196 m.p.h. I - 221 m.p.h. II - 210 m.p.h. III.
" " " 2,000 ft. 214 m.p.h. III.
" " " 5,000 ft. 215 m.p.h. I - 240 m.p.h. II.
" " " 6,000 ft. 242 m.p.h. II.
" " " 7,500 ft. 232 m.p.h. III.
" " " 9,000 ft. 231 m.p.h. III.
" " " 10,000 ft. 230 m.p.h. I - 255 m.p.h. II.
" " " 15,000 ft. 238 m.p.h. I - 257 m.p.h. II - 227 m.p.h. III.
" " " 20,000 ft. 218 m.p.h. III.
Cruising " 205 m.p.h. I - 230 m.p.h. II.
Stalling " 63 to 78 m.p.h. depending on flap settings.
Landing " 60 m.p.h. I - 64 m.p.h.
Climb rate. 1,500 ft./min. I - 2,000 ft./min. II - 1,485 ft./min. III.
" " to 15,000 ft. 13 mins. I - 9 mins. 50 secs. II - 10 mins. 30 secs. III.
" " " 20,000 ft. 21 mins. I - 17 mins. II - 16 mins. III.
Service ceiling. 28,000 ft. I - 25,100 ft. II - 27,300 ft. III.
" " absolute. 26,000 ft. II - 28,500 ft. III.
Range. 500 miles. I - 390 miles. II - 320 miles. III.
Duration economical. 1 hr. 45 mins. II eco. - 3 hrs. max.
Fuel capacity. 68 gallons. - Oil capacity. 7 gallons.
Take off run. 880 ft.
Landing run with flaps & brakes. 705 ft.

Dimensions
Span. 35 ft. 9 ins. I.
" 39 ft. II / III.
Length. 30 ft. 8 ins. I.
" 29 ft. 6 ins. II.
" 30 ft. 2 ins. III.
Height. 10 ft. I.
" 9 ft. 6 ins. II.
" 9 ft. 3 ins. III.
Wing area. 224 sq. ft. I.
" " 235 sq. ft. II / III.

Weights
Empty. 4,245 lbs. I - Loaded. 5,573 lbs. I.
" 4,130 lbs. II - " 5,312 lbs. II.
" 4,210 lbs. III - " 5,400 lbs. III.

MILES MASTER - *Picture above shows :- M.27 Mk.III's.*
Plan 9A >>>

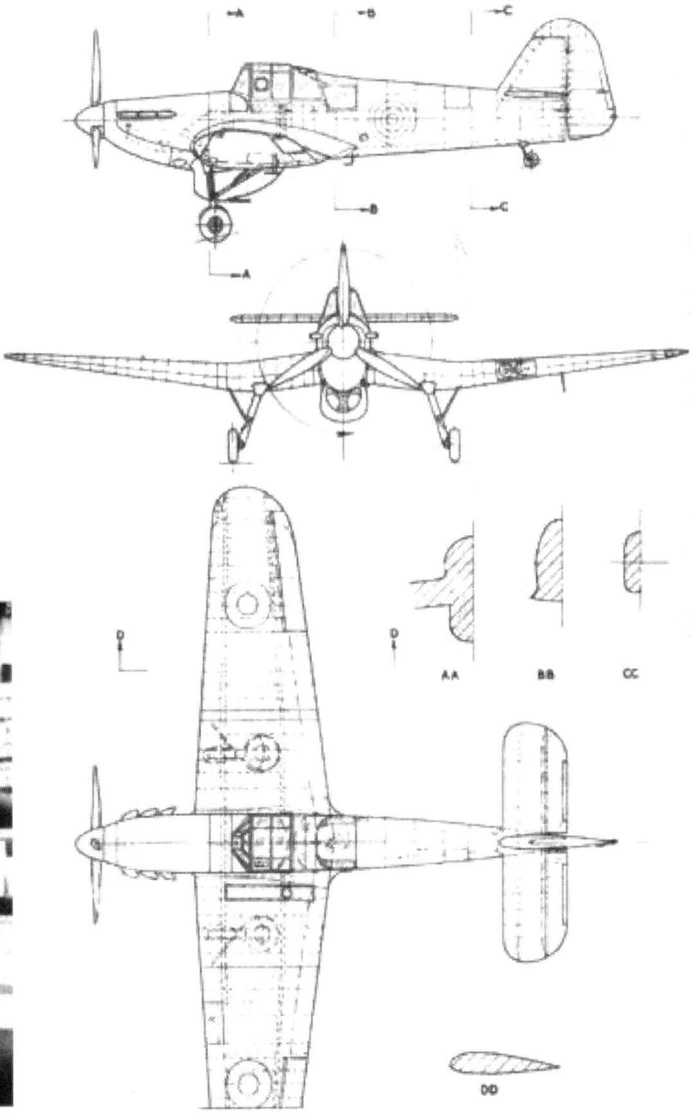

Master Fighter M.24. >>>

MILES M.11 WHITNEY STRAIGHT

A two seat side by side cabin monoplane, with a large luggage compartment.
Of a wooden construction, with a plywood and fabric covering.
The prototype - 290 / G-AECT - flew for the first time on the 14-5-1936.
Powered by 130 h.p. De Havilland Gipsy Major I four cylinder inverted in line engine.
M. 11 A - With modifications to the undercarriage and windscreen.
M. 11 B - One only - 305 / G-AERC - powered by 135 h.p. Villiers Maya I engine and used as a test bed by Villiers.
M. 11 C - Powered by 145 h.p. De Havilland Gipsy Major II engine, fitted with a variable pitch airscrew - 341 / U 4 / G-AEYI.
Many of the type were impressed during the Second World war.
Priced at £ 985 =

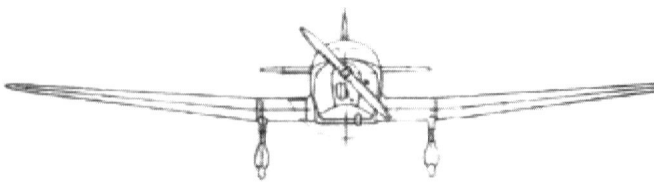

Nos. 290 / G-AECT - 303 / G-AENH / VH-ABN / ZK-AXN - 304 / G-AERS / ES 922 - 305 / G-AERC / AV 971 -
306 / OO-UMK / G-AFJJ / BD 168 - 307 / G-AERV / EM 999 / G-AERV - 308 / ZK-AEO / NZ 576 / ZK-AJF -
309 / G-AERY - 310 / G-AETB - 311 / ZK-AFH -
312 / G-AETS / DR 617 / G-AITM - 313 / G-AEUJ -
314 / G-AEUX / DJ 713 / G-AEUX / VP-KHO -
315 / G-AEUY / W 7422 - 316 / G-AEUZ / VP-KKF -
317 / G-AEVF / BS 814 -
318 / G-AEVA / DR 612 / G-AEVA -
319 / G-AEVG / DP 854 / DP 845 / G-AEVG / VH-EVG -
320 / G-AEWA / DJ 714 / G-AEWA - 321 / G-AEVH -
322 / G-AEVL / DP 855 / NF 751 / G-AEVL / ZK-AZX -
323 / ZK-AFG / NZ 571 / ZK-AJZ -
324 / G-AEVM / BS 815 - 325 / G-AEWK / AV 970 -
326 / G-AEWT / F-APPZ - 341 / U 4 / G-AEYI -
342 / G-AEYA / DP 237 - 343 / G-AEYJ / OO-ZUT -
344 / HB-URO - 345 / F-AQMA ? - 346 / G-AFAB / BD145 -
347 / G-AEZO - 348 / F-AQIK - 349 / HB-EPI -
350 / VH-UZA - 496 / F-AQCZ - 497 / G-AFBV -
499 / G-AFCC - 500 / G-AEYB / I-BONA -
501 / G-AEXJ / BS 818 - 502 / G-AFCN / V 4739 -
503 / ZK-AGB / NZ 577 / ZK-ALE - 505 / F-AQLX -
506 / U-0227 / G-AFZY / NF 747 / G-AFZY / ZK-AXD -
507 / G-AFJX / BD 183 / G-AFJX / ZK-AUK - 508 / F-AREQ -
509 / G-AFGK - VT-AKF / MA 944 - D-EKTR.

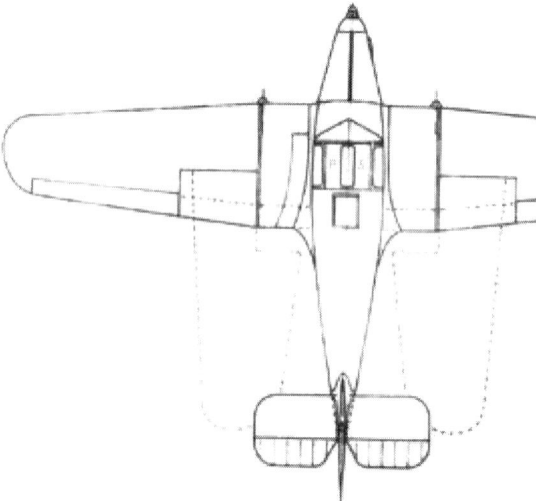

Performance
Maximum speed. 145 m.p.h. A - 155 m.p.h. B.
Cruising " 130 m.p.h. A - 136 m.p.h. B.
Landing " 38 m.p.h. A.
Climb rate. 850 ft./min. A - 1,050 ft./min. B.
Range cruising at 130 m.p.h. - 570 miles.
Fuel capacity. 30 gallons.
Dimensions
Span. 35 ft. 8 ins. - 17 ft. 2 ins. folded.
Length. 25 ft. - Height. 6 ft. 6 ins.
Wing area. 187 sq. ft.
Weights - Empty. 1,250 lbs. - Loaded. 1,896 lbs.

MILES M.12 MOHAWK

A dual controlled tandem two seat high performance long range cabin monoplane, built during 1936, to the specifications of Col. Charles Lindbergh.
Of a wooden construction, with a plywood and fabric covering.
One only - 298 / G-AEKW / HM 503 - flew for the first time on the 28-1-1937.
Powered by 200 h.p. Menasco Buccaneer B6-S six cylinder inverted in line air cooled supercharged engine.
Restored in 1946 and later converted to open cockpits.
Another was started upon - 301 / G-AEKX - but not completed.

Performance
Maximum speed. 190 m.p.h.
Cruising   "   170 m.p.h.
Landing   "   44 m.p.h.
Range. 1,400 miles.
Dimensions
Span. 35 ft. - Length. 25 ft. 6 ins.
Wing area. 183 sq. ft.
Weights
Empty. 1,605 lbs. - Loaded. 2,620 lbs.

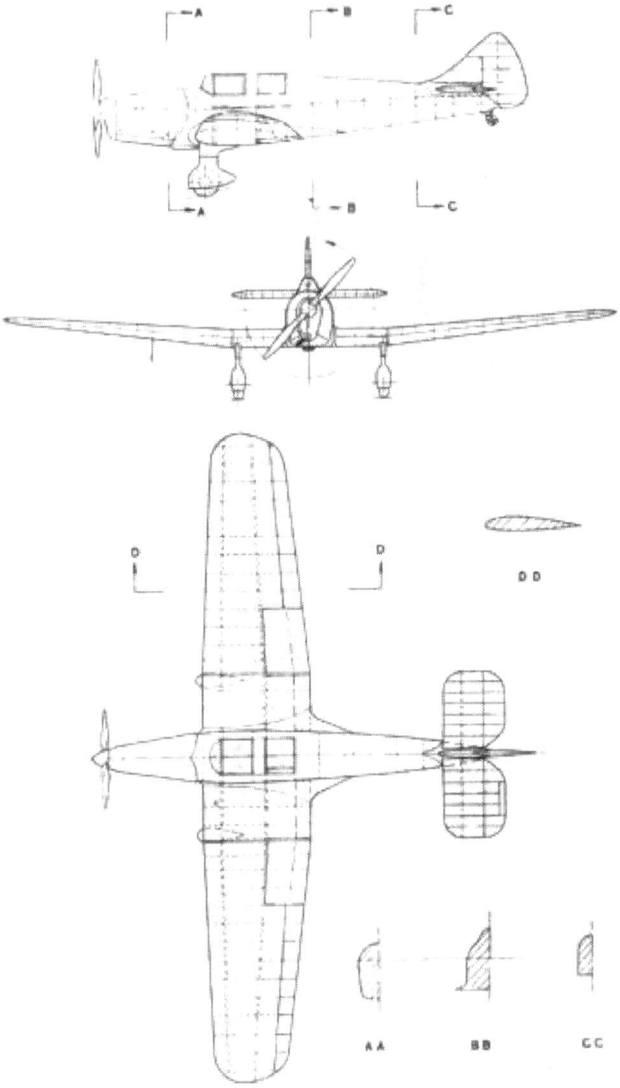

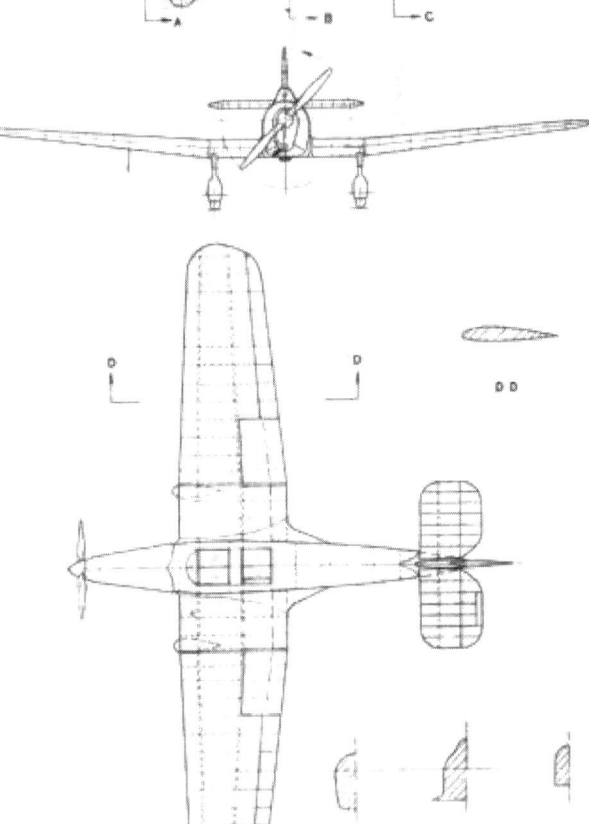

MILES   M.13   HOBBY

A small single seat racing / research aircraft, built for 1937 Kings Cup race.
Of a wooden construction, with plywood and fabric covering, also fitted with retractable undercarriage and hydraulically operated flaps.
One only - U 2 / G-AFAW / L 9706 - flew for the first time on the 4-9-1937.
Powered by 145 h.p. De Havilland Gipsy Major II four cylinder inverted in line air cooled engine, with a variable pitch airscrew.
It did not compete, as the re-tractable undercarriage was faulty and was sold later as a research aircraft.
Performance
Maximum speed. 207 m.p.h.
Dimensions
Span. 21 ft. 5 ins. - Length. 22 ft. 8 ins.
Height. 8 ft. 5 ins. - Wing area. 78 sq. ft.
Weights
Empty. 1,140 lbs. - Loaded. 1,527 lbs.

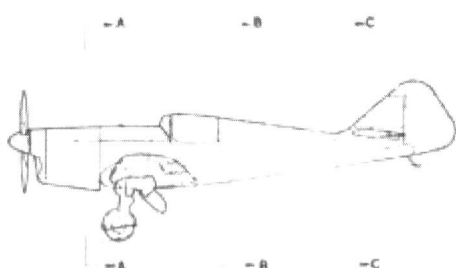

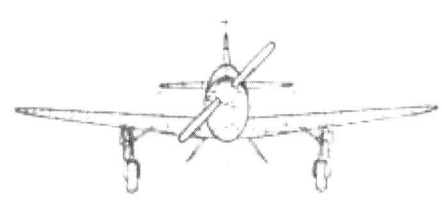

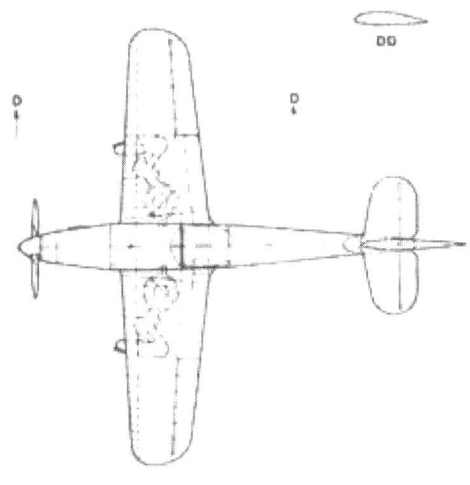

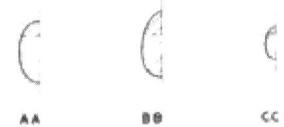

MILES M.14 MAGISTER

Spec. T. 40 / 36.

A two seat elementary training aircraft.
A development of the Hawk, but with larger cockpits and full blind flying equipment.
The fuselage is of spruce longerons and formers, which are plywood covered.
The wings have spruce and plywood spars and ribs, which are also plywood covered.
The tail unit is of a wooden framework and fabric covered.
Alloy castings were used on the stressed parts points.
The prototype appeared in 1937 and was the R.A.F.'s first monoplane trainer, entering service during October 1937.
Powered by 130 h.p. De Havilland Gipsy Major engine.

M. 14 A - HAWK TRAINER Mk. III - *Spec. T. 37 / 37.* - with modifications to the rear fuselage, tailplane and rudder.
Powered by 130 h.p. De Havilland Gipsy Major I engine or 155 h.p. Blackburn Cirrus Major III engine.
Production started with - L 5912 - and ended in 1941 with - V 1102 - after 1,293 had been built.

M. 14 B - HAWK TRAINER Mk. II - The prototype being - L 6913 / G-ANKA - powered by 135 h.p. Blackburn Cirrus Major II engine.
Nos. 494 / G-AEZP - 1078 / G-AFTR / BB 663 - 1079 / G-AFTS / BB 664.
L 6909 to L 6912 - L 6913 / G-AKNA
During the Second World War fifteen of the types were modified to carry 8 x 25 lb. bombs, in case the Germans landed on our beaches.
After the Second World War had ended, a great many of the surplus R.A.F Magister's were sold to the civilian market and various modifications were carried out.
Also served with the Fleet Air Arm, the Army and were built under licence in Turkey by Turk Hava Kurumu Ucak Fabrikasi.

Performance *Gipsy.*
Maximum speed at 1,000 ft. 145 m.p.h.
Cruising   "   120 m.p.h.
Stalling   "   52 m.p.h.
Landing   "   45 m.p.h.
Climb rate. 850 ft./min.
   "   " to 5,000 ft. 7 mins. 35 secs.
   "   "   " 10,000 ft. 18 mins. 45 secs.
Service ceiling. 17,000 ft.
Absolute   "   19,500 ft.
Range cruising at 110 m.p.h. 380 miles.
Duration. 3 hrs.
Fuel capacity. 21 1/2 gallons. - Oil capacity. 2 1/2 gallons.

Dimensions
Span. 33 ft. 10 ins. - Length. 24 ft. 7 1/2 ins.
Height. 6 ft. 8 ins. - Wing area. 172 sq. ft.

Weights
Empty. 1,286 lbs. - Loaded. 1,900 lbs.

MILES M.14 MAGISTER

Nos. 329 mock up - 331 / G-AETJ / ZK-AEX - 332 / G-AETL / ZK-AEY / ZK-ALO / NZ 586 -
333 / L 5912 / G-AGEO - 334 / L 5913 to 340 / L 5919 (L 5914 / G-AKML) -
351 / L 5920 to 358 / L 5927 (L 5921 / G-AJRU - L 5925 / G-AKPG) - 359 / L 6001 -
360 / L 5928 to 382 / L 5950 (L 5932 / G-AKXN) - 383 / L 5961 - 384 / L 5952 to 386 / L 5954 -
387 / L 5951 - 388 / L 5955 to 393 / L 5960 (L 5957 to Argentina) -
394 / L 5962 to 432 / L 6000 (L 5963 / G-AKMO - L 5971 / OO-MIC - L 5973 / G-AKKT - L 5977 / LV-XJS -
L 5983 / LR-AAL - L 5991 / G-AITU - L 5992 / G-AKMN - L 5993 / G-ALNZ - L 5999 / HB-EEB -
L 5966, 5976, 5978, 5982, L 5988, L 5990, L 5995, L 5998 to Argentina - L 5980 to Portugal -
L 5997 to Thailand) - 479 / VR-SAY - 480, to Russia -
486 to 493 (486 / ZK-AEZ / NZ 585 - 487 / ZK-AFA - 488, 489 to New Zealand - 490 / ZS-AMR -
491 / ZS-AMS - 492 / ZS-AMT - 493 / ZS-AMU for South Africa) -
494 / G-AEZP - 495 / G-AEZR - 511 / ZS-AMW / SAAF 1483 - 512 / ZS-AMY / SAAF 1485 -
513 / ZS-AMV - 514 / ZS-ALT -
515 / L 6894 to 537 / L 6916 (L 6896 / G-AIYL / F-OADV - L 6898, L 6900 to Argentina -
L 6903 to Irish Air Corps. - L 6909 to 6912 - L 6913 / G-AKNA - L 6914 not built replaced by N 4557) -
538 / G-AEZS / U 6 - 539 / G-AFBS / BB 661 - 540 & 541, to Egypt as L 201 & 202 -
542 / G-AFDB / BB 662 / 4557M - 543 to 546, to Egypt as L 203 to L 206 -
547 / A15-1 - 556 / G-AFET / AV 978 - 557 / G-AFEU - 558 / G-AFEV - 559 / G-AFEW -
560 / L 8051 to 599 / L 8090 (L 8053 to L 8056, L 8059, L 8061 / LV-XSF, L 8063 / LV-XML,
L 8072 / LV-XMW to Argentina - L 8058 / G-ALOA - L 8062 / LR-AAK to Lebanon - L 8068 / F-OAAQ -
L 8074 to Thailand - L 8075 / G-ALNY - L 8077 / F-BDPJ - L 8080 / G-AJGM - L 8082 / G-AKPM -
L 8083 / G-AIZL - L 8086 / G-AITV - L 8088 / CS-AFM to Portugal) -
600 / L 8091 / F-BDPP - 601 / L 8092 / G-AKMP - 602 / L 8093 to 604 / L 8095 -
605 / L 8127 to 627 / L 8149 (L 8127, L 8143, L 8149 to Argentina - L 8128 / G-AIUD - L 8135 / G-AIUB -
L 8138 / G-AITY / I-AITY - L 8145 / G-AKRI / EI-ADU) -
628 / N 2259 / G-AJHB - 629 / L 6917 - 630 / L 6918 - 631 / L 6919 - 632 / L 8151 - 633, to Egypt ? -
634 / L 207 to 637 / L 210, for Egypt - 639 / 159, to Estonia - 640 / N 4557 / G-ALIM -
642 / L 8152 to 666 / L 8176 (L 8160 / G-AJHD - L 8161, L 8169, L 8171, to Argentina - L 8176, to Portugal)-
667 / L 8200 to 704 / L 8237 (L 8204, F.A.A. - L 8206 / LV-XNF, L 8208, L 8213, L 8215 / LV-XNH,
L 8219 / LV-XOM, L 8229 / LV-XQQ, L 8225, L 8234 & L 8235 to Argentina - L 8210 / G-AHUL -
L 8211 / G-ALNX) -
705 / L 8249 to 751 / L 8295 (L 8250 / LV-XRT, L 8260, L 8266, L 8271, L 8272, L 8275, L 8278, L 8280,
L 8283, L 8289 / LV-XOL, L 8293 & L 8295 to Argentina - L 8256 / F-BDPK, L 8261 / F-BDPE,
L 8265 / F-BDPO, for France - L 8262 / G-ANWO - L 8274 / G-AKMT, to Egypt - L 8276 / G-ALOG -
L 8285 / G-AMMD / ZK-AWK - L 8288 / G-AJRT - L 8291, to Thailand) -
752 / L 8326 to 785 / L 8359 (L 8326 / G-AMBN - L 8339, L 8350, to Argentina -
L 8343 / 131, L 8352 / 137, to Irish Air Corps - L 8349 / G-AKMU -
L 8351 / G-AKMJ / ZS-DBF / VP-KIK / OO-CRU, to South Africa / Kenya & Belgium -
L 8353 / G-AMMC / ZK-AYW / L 8353, L 8357 / ZK-ANJ, to New Zealand - L 8358 / F-BDPL, to France -
L 8359 / G-AKRH) -
797 / YI-GFH, to Iraq - 798 / L220, to Egypt - 811 / L 8150 / LV-XOL, to Argentina -
812 / L 211 to 820 / L 219, for Egypt -
821 / N 3773 to 865 / N 3817 (N 3775 / G-AKPE - N 3777 / G-AJHE / F-OAFU,
N 3795 / G-AIUC / F-OAGQ / CN-TZE, N 3802 / F-BCDU, to France - N 3781, N 3785, N 3813, to Argentina -
N 3788 / G-ANLT - N 3793, to Thailand - N 3807, to Portugal - N 3816 / G-AKXM, to Egypt) -
866 / N 3820 to 907 / N 3861 (N 3821 / TF-BLU, to Iceland - N 3822 / G-AHYK - N 3825 / G-AKPL -
N 3827 / LV-XSG, N 3838, N 3841, N 3857, to Argentina - N 3830 / G-AJHC - N 3848 / F-BDPF, to France -
N 3850 / G-AJGN, to Egypt - N 3851 / G-AKMK / ZK-ATD, to New Zealand -
N 3856 / U-0252 / G-AGZR, to Thailand) -
908 / N 3862 / L 221 to 912 / N 3866 / L 225, for Egypt - 913 / N 3867, for Argentina - 914 / N 3868 -
915 / N 3869 / 130, for the Irish Air Corps. - 916 / N 3875 / L 226 to 920 / N 3879 / L 230, for Egypt -
921 / N 3880 to 925 / N 3884 (N 3880 & N 3883, to Argentina - N 3882 / G-AKOL -
926 / N 3885 / L 239 to 930 / N 3889 / L 243, for Egypt -
931 N 3890 to 935 / N 3894 (N 3890 / G-AKRW - N 3894 / ZK-ANK, for New Zealand -
936 N 3895 / L 231 to 940 / N 3899 / L 235, for Egypt -
941 / N 3900 to 952 / N 3911 (N 3901 / 75, for the Irish Air Corps. - N 3905 / LV-XPW, for Argentina) -
953 / N 3912 / L 236 to 955 / N 3914 / L 238, for Egypt -
956 / N 3918 to 983 / N 3945 (N 3918, N 3919, N 3920, N 3924, N 3928 & N 3930 to Argentina -
N 3925 / F-BDPC & N 3940 / F-BDPM, to France - N 3926 / G-ALOE / OO-ACH, to Belgium -
N 3933 / G-ALHB -
984 / 3951 to 1024 / N 3991 (N 3954 / G-AKKV - N 3955 / G-AIUG - N 3956, to Thailand - N 3962 / G-AIUE -
N 3967 / G-AJHH / F-OAFV & N 3969 / F-BDPB, to France - N 3972 / LV-XPN, N 3978, N 3985,
N 3991 to Argentina - N 3988 / G-AKUA) -

IN THE PILOT'S SEAT

The pilot's job looks easier when you follow the workings of the various controls.

1. Control stick 2. Rudder bar. 3. Tail trim wheel. 4. Ailerons. 5. Trailing centre wing flap. 6. Elevators. 7. Tail trim. 8. Rudder. 9. Tail trim operating cables. 10. Rudder operating cables. 11. Elevator operating cables. 12. Flap operating vacuum cylinder. 13. Aileron balance cable. 14. Aileron operating cable. 15. Pulleys.

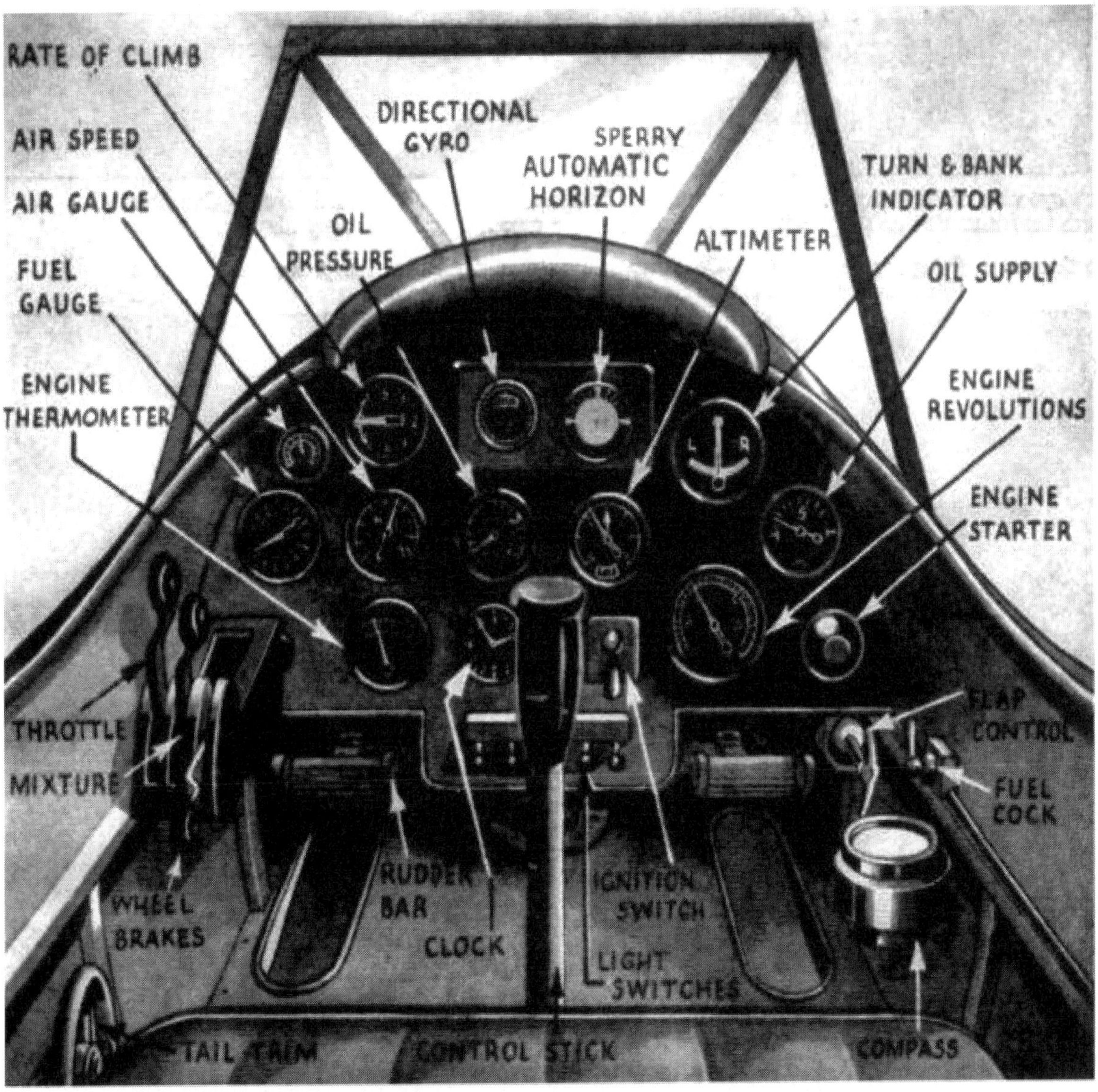

This diagram shows you the controls and indicators as they appear from the pilot's seat.

MILES M.14 MAGISTER

1025 / N 5389 / 31 to 1029 / N 5393 / 35, *for the Irish Air Corps.* - 1030 / N 5394 to 1035 / N 5399 - 1036 / N 5400 to 1040 / N 5404, *for the Irish Air Corps.* -
1041 / N 5405 to 1074 / N 5438 (*N 5406, N 5415 / LV-XMM, N 5423, N 5432, to Argentina - N 5408 / G-ALOB - N 5409, to Thailand - N 5418 / G-ALOC - N 5430 / G-ALOF - N 5438 / G-AITZ*) -
1078 / G-AFTR / BB 663 - 1079 / G-AFTS / BB 664 - 1080 / G-AFWY / BB 665 -
1081 / G-AFXA / BB 666 / G-ALOG / G-AFXA - 1082 / G-AFXB / BB 667 -
1083 / G-AFYV to 1086 / G-AFYY - *applications for registration cancelled.*
1611 / P 2374 to 1647 / P 2410 (*P 2388 / G-AMBM - P 2404 / G-AJZH - P 2406, P 2409, to Argentina - P 2408 / G-AIZJ*) -
1693 / P 2493 to 1710 / P 2510 *P 2493 / G-ALUW / OO-AJT, to Belgium - P 2500 / G-ALIO - P 2503, P 2504, to Argentina - P 2506 / G-AIZK*) -
1711 / P 6343 to 1750 / P 6382 (*P 6344 / G-AKMM, to Egypt - P 6355 / LV-RUX, P 6356, P 6371, P 6376, to Argentina - P 6366 / G-AICD - P 6367 / F-BDPH, to France - P 6369, to Thailand - P 6373, to Portugal - P 6374 / G-ALGK - P 6380 / G-AGVM - P 6382 / G-AJRS*) -
1751 / P 6396 to 1759 / P 6424 (*P 6396, P 6409 to Portugal - P 6402 / G-AMBP - P 6407 / G-AKJV - P 6410 / G-AKGS - P 6411 / G-AIDF - P 6412, P 6416, P 6417, to Argentina - P 6414 / 76, P 6422 / 77, P 6424 / 127, for the Irish Air Corps - P 6418, for Egypt - P 6419 / G-AJRV - P 6420 / G-AKNZ - P 6423 / F-BDPD, for France*) -
1780 / P 6436 to 1810 / P 6466 (*P 6438 / G-AIUF, for U.S.Army F.C. - P 6439 / F-BDPG, P 6441 / F-BDPA, for France - P 6440 / 74, for the Irish Air Corps. - P 6446 / G-AKKS - P 6488 , P 6451, P 6457 / LV-XRP, P 6464 / LV-XPT, for Argentina*) -
1811 / R 1810 to 1860 / R 1859 (*R 1815 / LV-XPZ, R 1828, R 1833, R 1846, R 1857, to Argentina - R 1819 / G-AKMR - R 1824 / G-ALIP - R 1825 / G-AITN - R 1826 / 128, R 1834 / 138, for the Irish Air Corps. - R 1831 / G-AHKP - R 1839 / G-AIYB - R 1841 / G-AITO - R 1842 / G-AITX, R 1844 / G-AITR, to Egypt - R 1847 / F-BDPN, to France - R 1853, to Thailand - R 1859 / G-AKRK*) -
1861 / R 1875 to 1910 / R 1924 (*R 1876 / G-AKRJ - R 1888 / G-AKRU - R 1893 / G-ALHA - R 1895, R 1896, R 1903 / LV-XQR, to Argentina - R 1898 / G-AITW, to Egypt - R 1901, R 1913 to Thailand - R 1907, to Turkey - R 1914 / G-AHUJ*) -
1911 / R 1940 to 1995 / R 1984 (*R 1950 / G-AHNW - R 1958, R 1982, to Argentina - R 1961 / G-AJSF - R 1962 / G-ALGL, R 1970 / G-AJGK, to Egypt - R 1963 / G-AJCM - R 1975 / OY-DNI, to Denmark - R 1976 / G-AKAU - R 1978 / G-AHNV - R 1983, to Thailand*) -
1956 / T 9669 to 1995 / T 9708 (*T 9669 / G-AMBO - T 9670, T 9671, T 9674, T 9675 / LV-XRJ, T 9690, T 9694 / LV-XMG, T 9704, to Argentina - T 9672 / G-AHUK - T 9684 / G-AKAS - T 9685 / G-AJHA - T 9686, T 9689, for Thailand - T 9692 / TF-REX, for Iceland - T 9695 / G-AKGR - T 9698 / G-AJJI - T 9705 / OO-NIC, to Belgium - T 9708 / G-AKKR / T 9967*) -
1996 / T 9729 to 2035 / T 9768 (*T 9730 / G-AITS - T 9732, T 9741, to Argentina - T 9733 / 129, to the Irish Air Corps. - T 9738 / G-AKAT - T 9744, T 9761, to Thailand - T 9755 / G-AGEO - T 9758 / G-ALOH - T 9759 / OY-ABI / SE-CGF, to Denmark / Sweden - T 9760 / G-ALIN - T 9766 / G-AHNU - T 9768 / G-AIUA*) -
2036 / T 9799 to 2085 / T 9848 (*T 9799, T 9810, T 9819, T 9822, T 9825, T 9828, T 9838, T 9840, T 9848 / LV-XPF, to Argentina - T 9801, T 9815, to Portugal - T 9802 / G-AKKX - T 9803 / 135, T 9807 / 132, to the Irish Air Corps. - T 9804 / F-BDPI, T 9812 / G-AICE / F-OAPJ, to France - T 9805 / G-AKRL / OO-PAB, to Belgium - T 9809, to Thailand - T 9826 / G-ALFH - T 9834 / G-AHYL - T 9841 / G-AKKY - T 9844 / G-AJHF - T 9848 / G-AHYM*) -
2086 / T 9869 to 2135 / T 9918 (*T 9869, to Portugal - T 9870 / G-AIYC - T 9876 / G-AKRV - T 9883 / G-AKRT - T 9887 / G-AKRM - T 9888 / G-AIOJ / ZK-ATE, to New Zealand - T 9889 / G-ALGJ - T 9896 / G-AKRV / VP-KNW - T 9899, T 9900, T 9903, to Turkey - T 9910, T 9911, to Argentina - T 9915 / G-AIYD*) -
2136 / T 9943 to 2175 / T 9982 (*T 9946, T 9959, T 9963 / LV-XSH, to Argentina - T 9955 / G-AIOK - T 9957 / G-ALGZ - T 9967 / G-AKKR - T 9976 / G-AJDR - T 9977 / G-AHNE / ZK-BBA, to New Zealand*) -
2176 / V 1003 to 2215 / V 1042 (*V 1008, V 1020, V 1039, V 1040 / LV-XSD, to Argentina - V 1016 / 134, to the Irish Air Corps. - V 1018 / G-AKMY -*
2216 / V 1063 to 2255 / V 1102 (*V 1063 / LV-XMR, V 1082, V 1085 / LV-XQT, V 1088, to Argentina - V 1074 / G-AKKZ - V 1075 / G-AKPF - V 1086 / G-ALFE - V 1089 / 133 & V 1094 / 136, to the Irish Air Corps.*

MILES M.14 MAGISTER

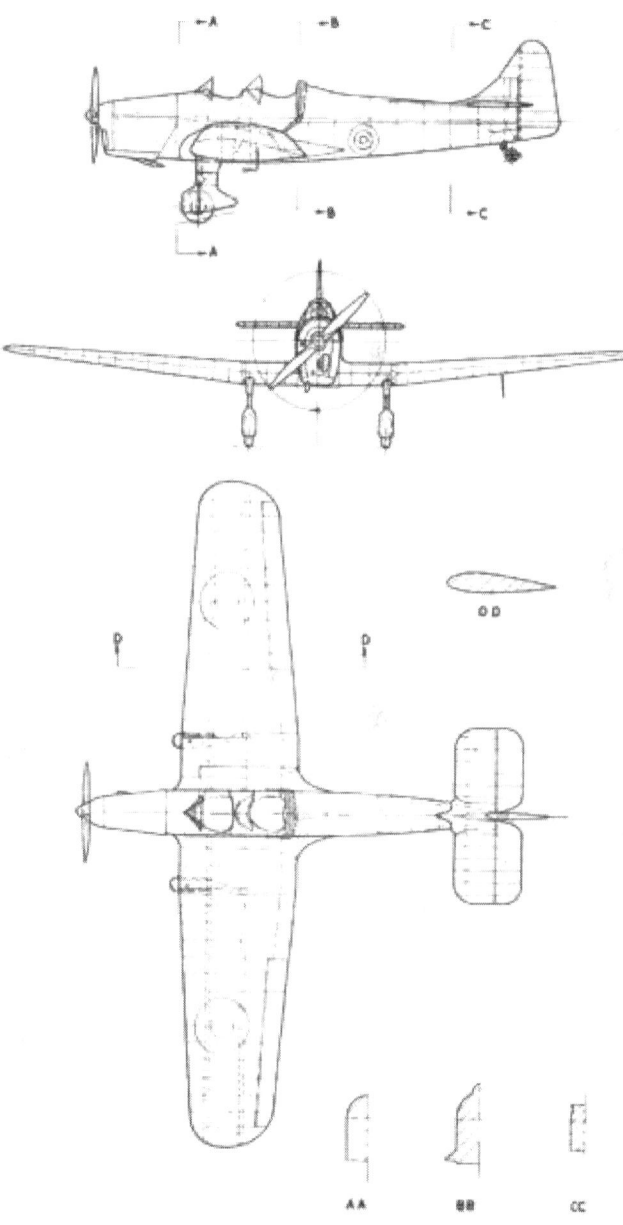

MILES M.15

A two seat elementary training monoplane aircraft.
Of a wooden construction, with plywood and fabric covering.
Powered by 200 h.p. De Havilland Gipsy Six six cylinder inverted in line air cooled engine.
Two prototypes built to - *Spec. T. 1 / 37* - as trainers for the R.A.F.
The first - 641 / L 7714 - flew for the first time on the 4-2-1939 and the second one was -
1077 / U 0234 / P 6326 - not completed.
Unsatisfactory, no further development.

Dimensions
Span. 33 ft. 5 ins. - Length. 29 ft. 6 ins.
Height. 10 ft. 5 ins. - Wing area. 200 sq. ft.

Weights
Empty. 1,830 lbs. - Loaded. 2,530 lbs.

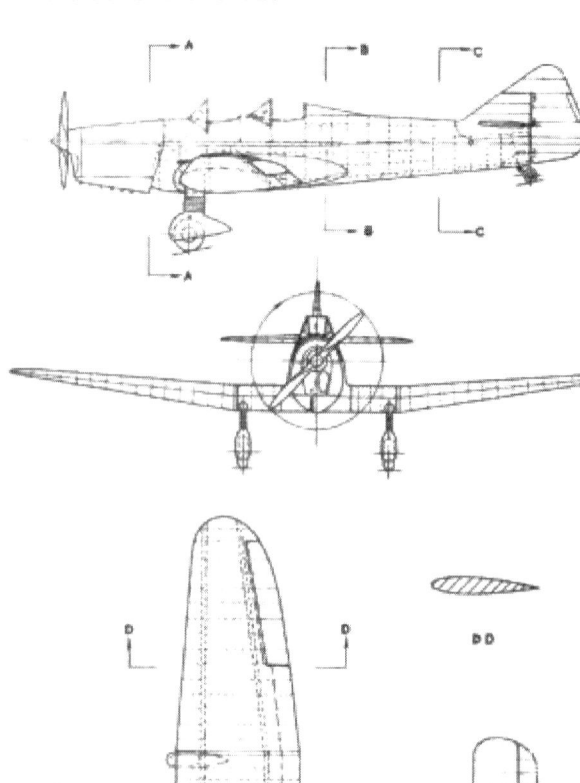

MILES M.16 MENTOR

Spec. 38 / 37.

A two / three seat dual controlled light cabin monoplane, with doors on both sides.
For day or night training, communications duties and radio instruction.
Of a wooden construction, with plywood and fabric covering.
The prototype flew for the first time on the 5-1-1938, powered by 200 h.p. De Havilland Gipsy Six engine.
A total of forty five were delivered to the R.A.F. from 1938 until mid-1939 and some were still in service during 1944.
Nos. 434 / L 4392 to 478 / L 4436 - (L 4420 / G-AHKM).

Performance
Maximum speed. 156 m.p.h.
Landing   "   53 m.p.h.
Climb rate. 780 ft./min.
Service ceiling. 13,800 ft.

Dimensions
Span. 34 ft. 9 1/2 ins. - Length. 26 ft. 1 3/4 ins.
Height. 9 ft. 8 ins. - Wing area. 181 sq. ft.

Weights
Empty. 1,978 lbs. - Loaded. 2,710 lbs.

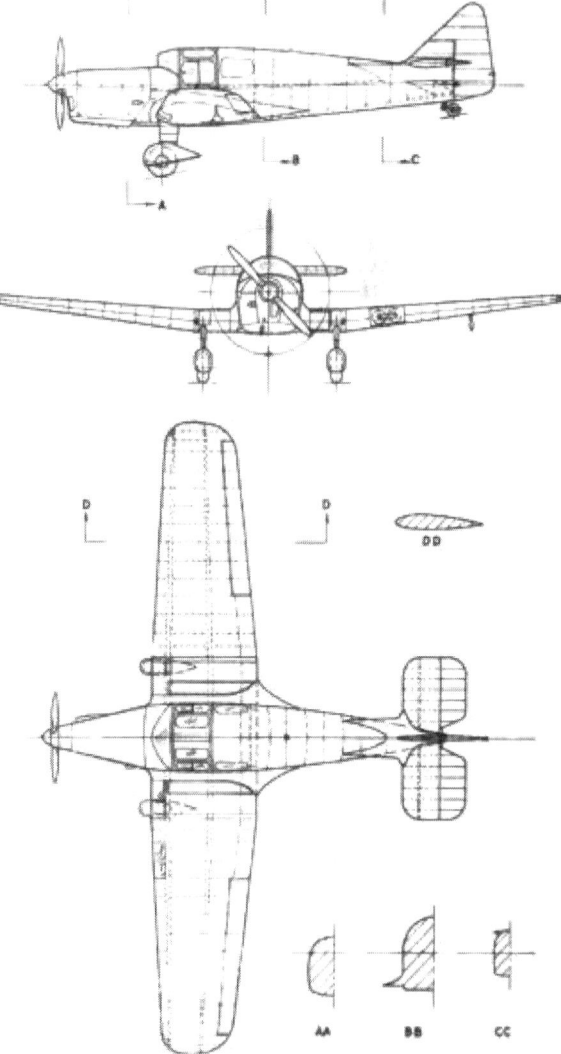

MILES   M.17   MONARCH

A two / three seat light commercial cabin monoplane, a development of the M.11 Whitney Straight.
Of a wooden construction, with plywood and fabric covering.
A one piece moulded perspex windscreen was fitted, plus dual controls and with the door on the starboard side.
The prototype - G-AFCR - flew for the first time on the 21-2-1938, and eleven of the type were produced, between 1938 / 39.
Powered by 130 h.p. De Havilland Gipsy Major I four cylinder inverted in line air cooled engine.
Nos. 638 / G-AFCR / W 6461 - 786 / G-AFGL / F-ARPE - 787 / OO-UMK / TP 819 / U-0226 / G-AGFW - 789 / G-AFJU / X 9306 - 790 / G-AFJZ / W 6462 - 792 / G-AFLW - 793 / G-AFRZ / W 6463 / G-AIDE - 795 / G-AFTX (+ 3 unknown).
Many were impressed during the Second World War for communications duties and some were still around in 1944.
Priced at £ 1,250 =

Performance
Maximum speed. 145 m.p.h.
Cruising   "   130 m.p.h.
Landing   "   45 m.p.h.
Climb rate. 850 ft./min.
Service ceiling. 17,400 ft.
Range. 620 miles on 30 gallons - duration 4 hrs 30 mins.
   "   910   "   " 44   "   -   "   7 " 15   "

Dimensions
Span. 35 ft. 7 ins. - Length. 25 ft. 11 3/4 ins.
Height. 8 ft. 9 1/4 ins. - Wing area. 180 sq. ft.

Weights
Empty. 1,390 lbs. - Loaded. 2,150 lbs.

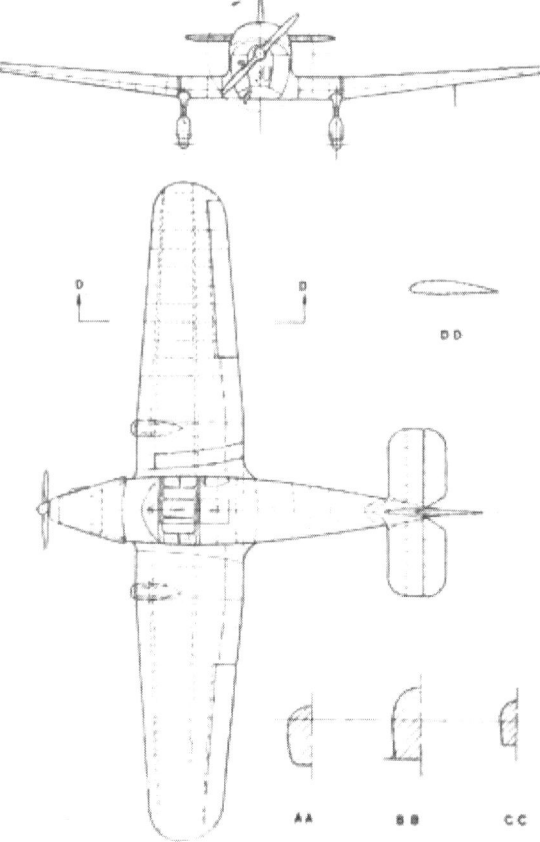

MILES M.18

A two seat tandem elementary training monoplane, with dual controls, designed by W.Capley.
The intended replacement for the Magister and similar in construction.

Mk. I - The prototype - 1075 / U 2 / U 0222 / G-AFRO - flew for the first time on the 4-12-1938 and initially with tail wheeled undercarriage.
Powered by 130 h.p. De Havilland Gipsy Major III four cylinder inverted in line air cooled engine or 150 h.p. Blackburn Cirrus Major four cylinder in line inverted air cooled engine.
The prototype was modified to a single seater, also flown with three wheeled undercarriage - U 0222 - also as a glider.
The aircraft was also fitted with the experimental 110 h.p. Jameson FF engine, during 1946 / 47.
The aircraft was accepted as satisfactory by the Air Ministry and was ordered into production twice, but each time it was cancelled.

Mk. II - U 8 / U 0224 / HM 545 / G-AHKY - flew for the first time during November 1939.
Powered by 150 h.p. Blackburn Cirrus Major III engine.
Modifications to the tail, fin and rudder moved forward 22 ins.

Mk. III - 4432 / U 0238 / U 3 / G-AHOA - with an enclosed cabin and flew for the first time during October 1942.
Powered by 150 h.p. Blackburn Cirrus Major III engine, *specs. as Mk.II.*

M. 18 H.L - U 0236 / JN 703 - A research aircraft for the R.A.E., which flew for the first time during December 1942.
Powered by 150 h.p. Blackburn Cirrus Major engine.
Fitted with an experimental high lift wing, on which the wing span varied from 31 ft. to 22 ft. depending on research.

Performance
Maximum speed. 140 m.p.h. I - 130 m.p.h. II.
Cruising   "   125 m.p.h. I - 120 m.p.h. II.
Stalling   "   50 / 56 m.p.h.
Landing   "   42 m.p.h.
Climb rate. 1,000 ft./min.
  "   " to 5,000 ft. 8 mins.
  "   " " 10,000 ft. 22 mins.
Service ceiling. 12,400 ft. - 14,100 ft. absolute.
Range. 376 miles.
Duration. 3 hrs. 15 mins.
Fuel capacity. 24 gallons.
Oil   "   2 1/2 "

Dimensions
Span. 31 ft. - 30 ft. HL.
Length. 24 ft. 10 ins. - Height. 9 ft. 4 ins.
Wing area. 183.2 sq. ft. - 147 sq. ft. HL.

Weights
Empty. 1,180 lbs. I - 1,306 lbs. II - 1,420 lbs. HL.
Loaded. 1,800 lbs. I - 1,925 lbs. II - 2,000 lbs. HL.

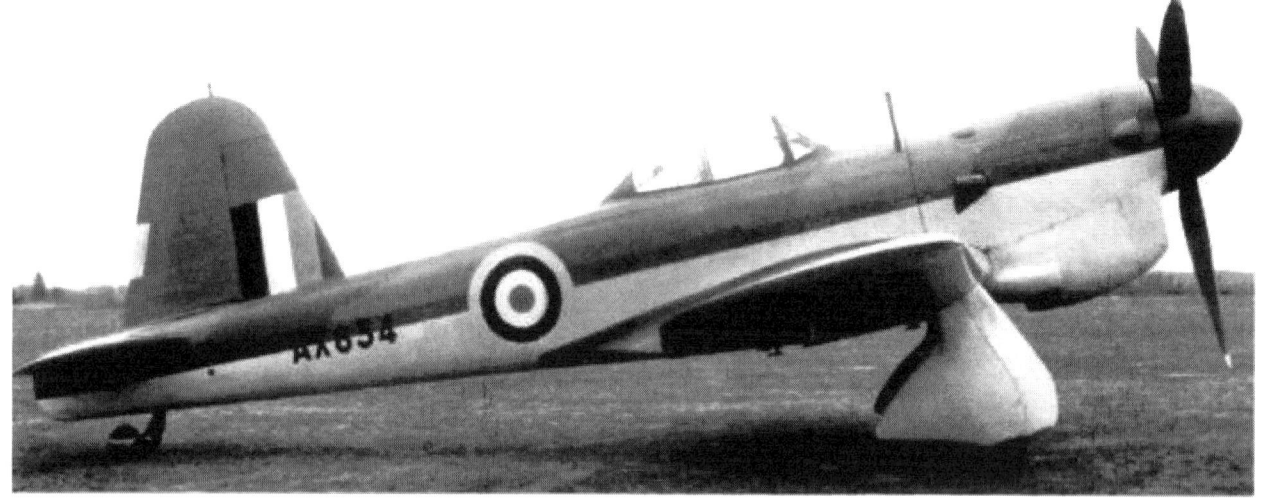

MILES M.20

Spec. F. 19 / 40

A single seat twelve gun fighter monoplane aircraft of 1940, designed by Walter Capley.
Designed, built and flown in sixty five days, flying for the first time on the 14-9-1940.
Of a wooden construction, using many parts from the Miles Master and fitted with a fixed undercarriage.
Powered by 1,300 h.p. Rolls-Royce Merlin XX twelve cylinder water cooled supercharged Vee engine.
Armed with twelve 0.303 Browning machine guns outboard of the centre section, plus 5,000 rounds of ammunition.
Only two built - AX 834 & U-0228 / DR 616, as a Naval Fighter type, *Spec. N. 1 / 41*.
Should there be a need for our fighter aircraft to be replaced quickly, due to the losses during the Battle of Britain, which may have been excessive and the majority of our fighter aircraft being lost.
This was to have possibly been a very quick replacement aircraft, a stand by, a back up, just in case the need should arise.
Available, but in the event, not required.

Performance
Maximum speed. 350 m.p.h.
Climb rate. 3,200 ft./min.
Service ceiling. 31,400 ft. - 35,500 ft. absolute.
Range. 550 miles. eco. - 870 miles. max.
Duration. 2 hrs. to 5 hrs. max.
Fuel capacity. 150 gallons.

Dimensions
Span. 34 ft. 7 ins. - Length. 30 ft. 1 ins.
Height. 12 ft. 6 ins. - Wing area. 235 sq. ft.

Weights
Empty. 5,870 lbs. - Loaded. 7,760 lbs.

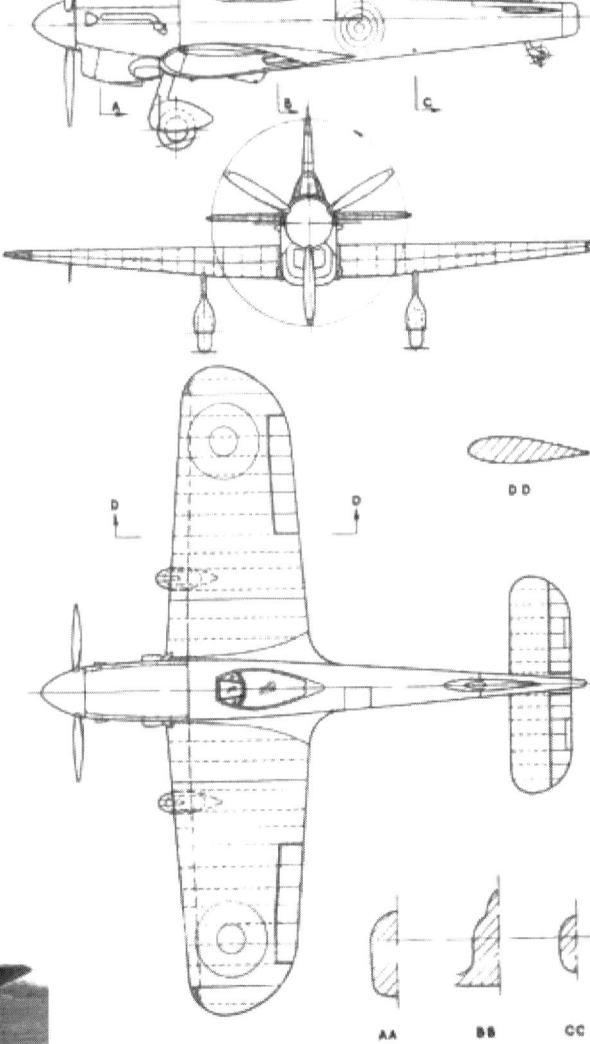

MILES M.25 MARTINET   Spec. 12/41.
MILES M.50 QUEEN MARTINET   " Q. 10/43.

A two seat target tug, of a wooden construction, which is plywood and fabric covered.
Two prototypes - LR 241 - which flew for the first time on the 24-4-1942 and - LR 244.
Martinet T.T.Mk. I - The first aircraft to join the R.A.F. designed specifically from the start as a target tug.
Powered by 870 h.p. Bristol Mercury XX or XXX nine cylinder radial engine.
Both types of winch could be fitted, motor or wind driven and can carry six flag and sleeve drogue targets.
Also carried two way radio, dinghy, parachute stowage and desert equipment if required.
A production batch of 235 aircraft :- Nos. EM 410 to EM 420 - EM 434 to EM 481 - EM 496 to EM 532 - EM 545 to EM 593 - EM 613 to EM 662 - EM 677 to EM 716.
A second production batch of 400 aircraft :- Nos. HN 861 to HN 894 - HN 907 to HN 916 - HN 938 to HN 984 - HP 114 to HP 149 - HP 163 to HP 183 - HP 199 to HP 227 - HP 241 to HP 288 - HP 303 to HP 335 - HP 348 to HP 393 - HP 405 to HP 448 - HP 464 to HP 496 - HP 510 to HP 528.
A third production batch of 200 aircraft :- Nos. JN 273 to JN 309 - JN 416 to JN 460 - JN 485 to JN 513 - JN 538 to JN 555 - JN 580 to JN 601 - JN 634 to JN 682.
A fourth production batch of 355 aircraft :- Nos. MS 499 to MS 535 - MS 547 to MS 590 - MS 602 to MS 647 - MS 659 to MS 705 - MS 717 to MS 759 - MS 771 to MS 820 - MS 832 to MS 876 - MS 889 to MS 931.
A fifth production batch of 300 aircraft :- Nos. NR 293 to NR 336 - NR 349 to NR 390 - NR 405 to NR 446 - NR 460 to NR 503 - NR 516 to NR 556 - NR 569 to NR 616 - NR 628 to NR 666.
A sixth production batch of 125 aircraft :-
Nos. PW 947 to PW 988 - PX 101 to PX 147 - PX 163 to PX 198.
A seventh production batch of 300 aircraft :- Nos. RG 882 to RG 929, *for the R.A.F.* - RH 113 to RH 121, *for the Royal Navy* - (*The majority of the next part of the batch were for the R.A.F. as Queen Martinets*) - RH 193 to RH 205, cancelled - RH 218 to RH 259, cancelled - RH 273 to RH 315, cancelled - RH 329 to RH 365, cancelled.
Civilian types :-
Nos. EM 646 / G-AJJL / SE-BCO - HN 913 / G-AJJO / SE-BCN - HP 145 / G-AJJK / SE-BCP - MS 836 / G-AJZB - MS 871 / G-AJZC.
A total of 1,724 were produced.

Performance
Maximum speed at sea level. 222 m.p.h.
 "   "   " 6,000 ft. 240 m.p.h.
 "   "   " 10,000 ft. 238 m.p.h.
 "   "   " 15,000 ft. 235 m.p.h.
Cruising   " 200 m.p.h.
Landing   "   60 m.p.h.
Climb rate to 5,000 ft. 3 mins. 30 secs.
 "   "   " 10,000 ft. 8 mins.
Range. 694 miles.
Duration. 5 hrs.
Fuel capacity. 130 gallons.
Oil   "   8 1/2   "

Dimensions
Span. 39 ft.
Length. 30 ft. 11 ins.
Height. 11 ft. 7 ins.
Wing area. 238 sq. ft.

Weights
Empty. 4,559 lbs.
Loaded. 6,680 lbs. 25.
 "   6,500 lbs. 50.

Allocations
A.S.R. - No. 269.
A.A.C. - Nos. 285, 286, 287, 289, 290, 291, 567, 577, 587, 595, 598, 631, 639, 679, 691 & 695.
F.A.A. - Nos. 722, 723, 725, 726, 728, 733, 770, 771, 775, 776, 789, 792 & 794.

Picture above shows :- Queen Martinet - RH 123.

MILES MARTINET + QUEEN MARTINET

QUEEN MARTINET - A radio controlled pilotless target version, also powered by the 870 h.p. Bristol Mercury engine.
The prototype - PW 979 - on which work began during 1943 and 65 Queen Martinets, starting with - RH 122 - followed into production.
The type made its first public appearance at Farnborough during 1946.
A glider tug version was also produced and they remained in service until approx. 1952.
Nos. HN 909 - HN 945 - HP 222 - HP 272 - HP 310 - JN 590 - MS 515 - MS 723 - MS 730 - MS 741 - MS 847 - NR 387 - NR 599 - PW 979 - *Part of 7th. production batch, for the R.A.F. :-*
RH 122 to RH 148 - RH 162 to RH 168 - RH 170 to RH 181 - RH 183 - RH 184 - RH 187 to RH 192 - *Part of the 7th. production batch, for the Royal Navy :-* RH 169 - RH 182 - RH 185 - RH 186.
A production batch of 11 aircraft :- Nos. VF 110 to VF 120.

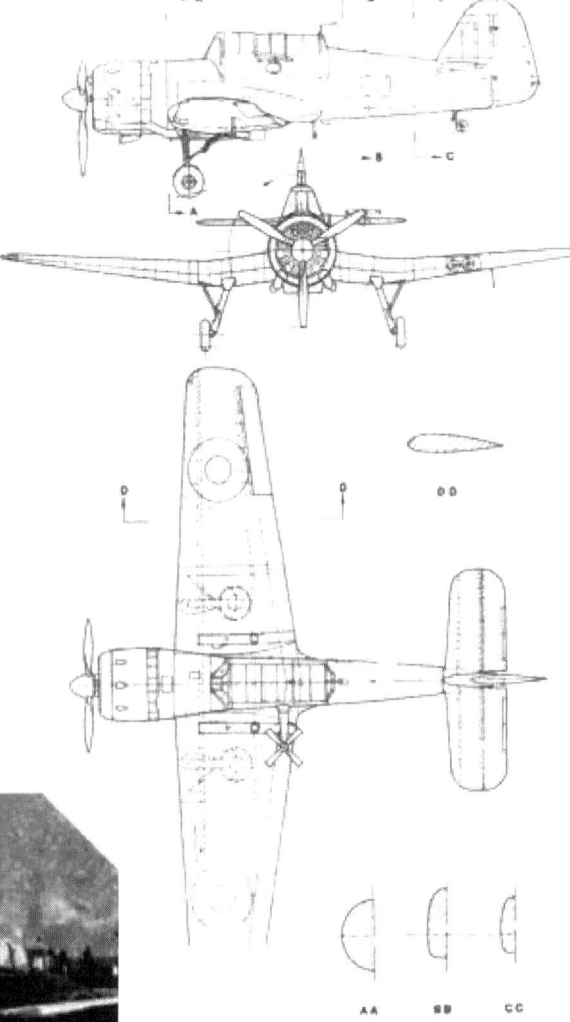

MILES M.28

Designed by F.G.Miles and built during 1942, as a private venture.
As a three or four seat light commercial cabin monoplane, or as a side by side two seat cabin monoplane, for use as an elementary or intermediate training or communications aircraft.
The aircraft can be used as an ambulance, light freighter, army co-operation duties, etc.
Of an all wooden construction and plywood and fabric covered, also fitted with retractable undercarriage.
Six of the type were produced, the first of these flying for the first time on the 11-7-1941.
Mk. I - U 0232 - Powered by 130 h.p. De Havilland Gipsy Major four cylinder inverted in line air cooled engine, with fixed pitch airscrews.
No rear window and was later dismantled during 1942.
The rear fuselage and tail unit was used as the M.38 Messenger prototype.
Mk. II - No. U 0237 / HM 583 / G-AJVX, in 1947 / VH-BBK, in 1951.
Powered by 140 h.p De Havilland Gipsy Major IIA engine, with a fixed pitch propeller and dual controls.
Later as - G-AJVX - powered by 140 h.p. Blackburn Cirrus Major III engine, with fixed-pitch airscrews.
Mk. III - A three seat trainer, with a thinner centre section and triple controls -
4684 / U 0242 / PW 397 / G-AISH - built during 1943 and scrapped in February 1948.
Powered by 150 h.p. Blackburn Cirrus Major III engine
Mk. IV - A four seat touring monoplane, built during 1944.
One only - 4685 / U 0243 / G-AGVX / HB-EED / VH-AKH / VH-AKC.
Powered by 145 h.p. De Havilland Gipsy Major II A engine.
Mk. V - A four seater, with a square rear window and revised undercarriage, built during 1947.
One only - 6697 / G-AJFE / HB-EEF - powered by 150 h.p. Blackburn Cirrus Major III engine, with a fixed pitch propeller.
Mk. VI - One only - 6268 / G-AHAA / D-EHAB - built during 1946.
As Mk.V, other than oval rear window.

Performance
Maximum speed. 155 m.p.h. I / II / III - 158 m.p.h. IV.
Cruising " 135 m.p.h. I / II / III - 139 m.p.h. IV.
Landing " 42 m.p.h.
Climb rate. 950 ft./min. I / II - 1,250 ft./min. III - 1,400 ft./min. IV.
" " to 10,000 ft. 14 mins.
Range. 700 miles. I / II / III - 715 miles. III.
Duration. 5 hrs. I / II - 4 hrs. 45 mins. III - 4 hrs. 20 mins. IV.
Fuel capacity. 24 gallons.
Oil " 2 1/2 "

Weights
Empty. 1,400 lbs. I / II - 1,480 lbs. III -
" 1,425 lbs. III - 1,460 lbs. IV.
Loaded. 2,400 lbs. I / II - 2,500 lbs. III / IV.

Dimensions
Span. 30 ft. 8 ins. - Length. 24 ft.
Height. 8 ft. 4 ins. - Wing area. 162 sq. ft.

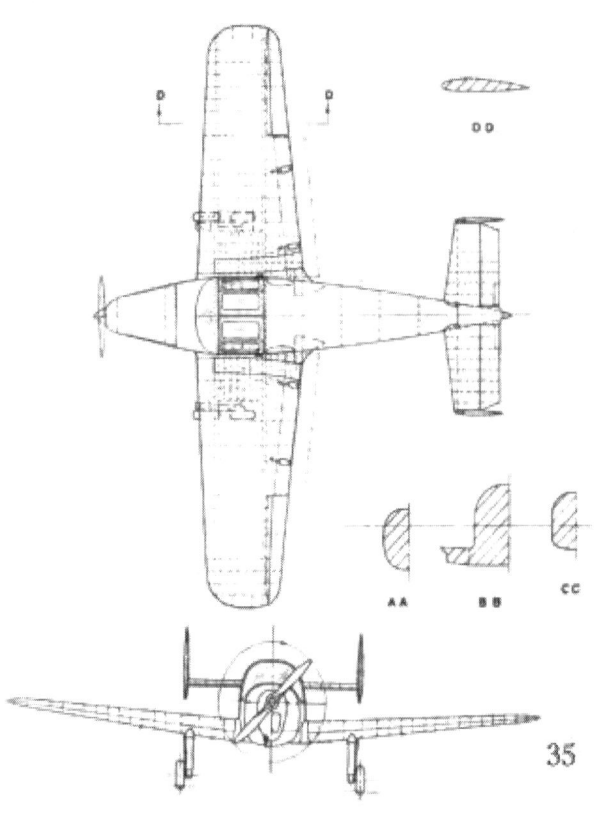

MILES M.30 'X' MINOR

A two seat experimental research cabin monoplane, with an aerofoil fuselage and retractable tricycle undercarriage.
Of a wooden construction, plywood and fabric covered.
Powered by two 130 h.p. De Havilland Gipsy Major four cylinder inverted in line air cooled engines.
Flew for the first time during February 1942.

Performance
Maximum speed. 160 m.p.h.
Landing   "   60 m.p.h.

Dimensions
Span. 33 ft. - 38 ft. 6 ins. with wing extensions.
Length. 26 ft. 3 ins. - Height. 9 ft. 0 1/2 ins.
Wing area. 200 sq. ft.

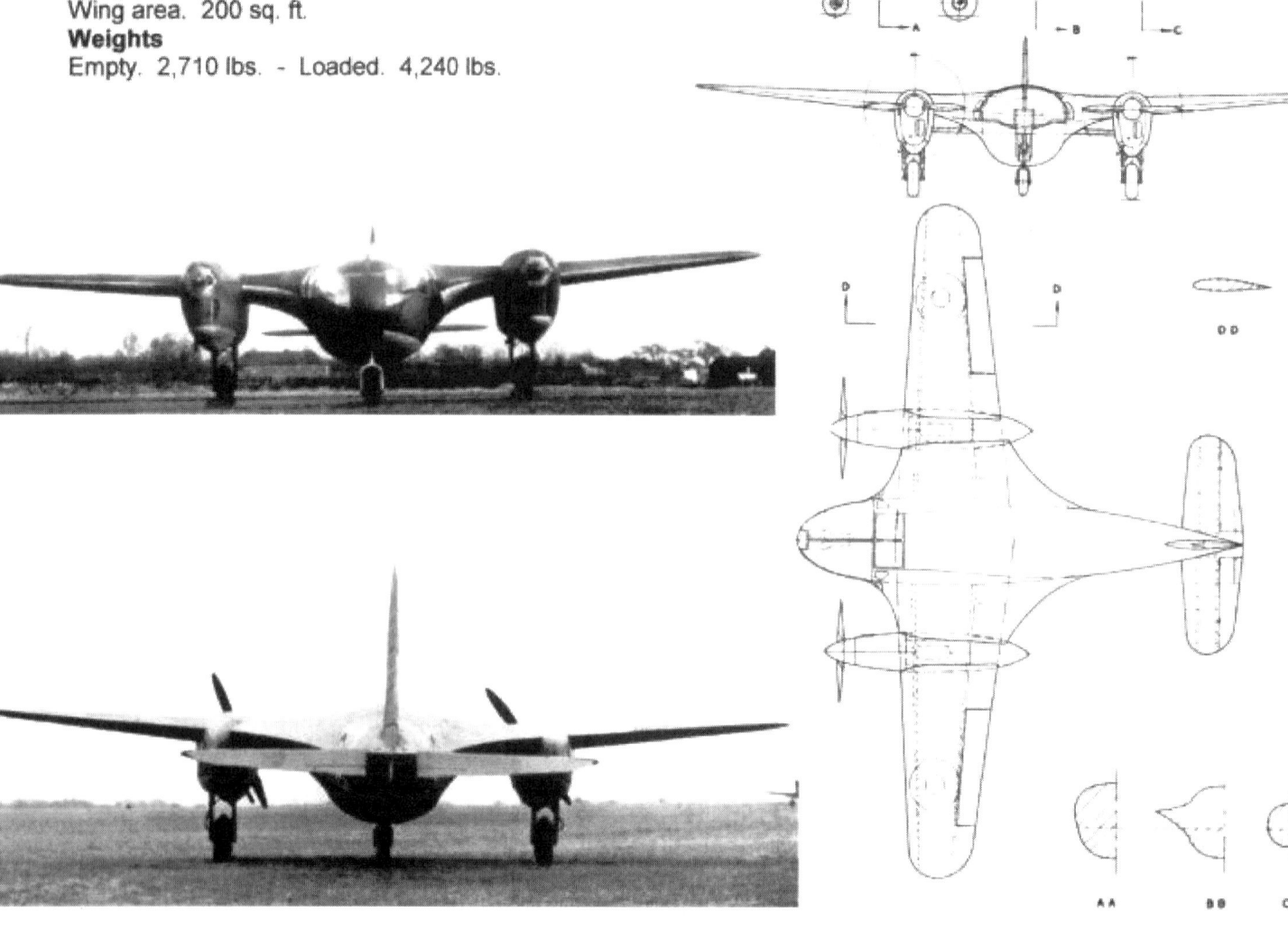

Weights
Empty. 2,710 lbs. - Loaded. 4,240 lbs.

MILES M.33 MONITOR

Spec. Q. 9/42.

A high speed target tug, with a crew of two.
The Monitor was also the first twin engined aircraft that was specifically designed as a target tug, to enter service.
The fuselage and tail unit are of an all metal stressed skin construction.
The wings are of a wooden construction and are plywood covered.
The prototype - NF 900 - flew for the first time on the 5-4-1944, but was later destroyed in a crash.
Two more prototypes were built - NP 402 & NP 405.
Powered by two 1,750 h.p. Wright Cyclone R-2600-31 Double-Row fourteen cylinder radial engines.
The initial requirements for the R.A.F. for an aircraft capable of towing 16 ft. or 32 ft. wing span targets and drones at 300 m.p.h. for between 3 to 4 hrs. was abandoned.
T.T.Mk. I - For the R.A.F., which was later abandoned.
The Royal Navy required an aircraft to be able to simulate dive bomb attacks on warships at speeds of around 400 m.p.h.
T.T.Mk. II - For the F.A.A., modifications to the aircraft, including the hydraulic winch and the fitting of hydraulic dive brakes
The first entering service with the Royal Navy during the Autumn of 1945.
Four hundred were ordered but only twenty aircraft were built and not all were completed.
Ten were delivered and the last ten were broken up as they were no longer required, due to the end of the Second World war.
Nos. NP 406 to NP 425.

Performance
Maximum speed at 20,000 ft. 360 m.p.h.
Cruising   "   300 m.p.h.
Climb rate. 2,480 ft./min.
    "   " to 10,000 ft. 5 mins.
    "   "   " 15,000 ft. 6 mins. 25 secs.
    "   "   " 20,000 ft. 10 mins. 5 secs.
Service ceiling. 29,000 ft.
Range. 1,000 miles. - 2,750 miles max.
Fuel capacity. 480 gallons.
Oil   "   32   "

Dimensions
Span. 56 ft. 3 ins. - Length. 47 ft. 8 ins.
Height. 14 ft. 3 ins. - Wing area. 500 sq. ft.

Weights
Empty. 15,723 lbs.
Loaded. 21,000 lbs. I - 21,056 lbs. II.

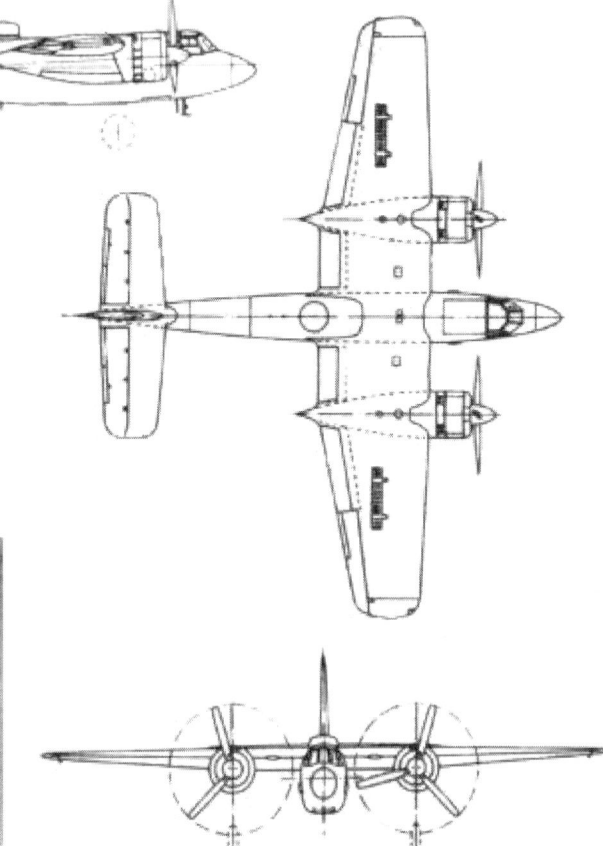

MILES   LIBELLULA   M.35

A private venture for a single seat tandem wing research aircraft, as a projected carrier based fighter, during 1941.
Of a wooden construction, with plywood and fabric covering.
Both sets of wings were equipped with flaps and the four wheel undercarriage was fixed, the fourth wheel being added as protection for the propeller on landing.
Powered by a 130 h.p. De Havilland Gipsy Major four cylinder inverted in line air cooled pusher engine behind the rear wing.
Flown by F.G.Miles during May 1942, initially unstable but later cured.
Not required.
(Libellula, a member of the Dragonfly insect family - entomological).

Performance
Fuel capacity. 15 gallons.
Oil   "   4   "

Dimensions
Span. 20 ft. front   - 20 ft. 5 ins. rear.
Length. 20 ft. 4 ins.
Height. 6 ft. 9 ins.
Front wing area. 50 sq. ft.
Rear   "   "   84.5 sq. ft.

Weights
Empty. 1,460 lbs. - Loaded. 1,850 lbs.

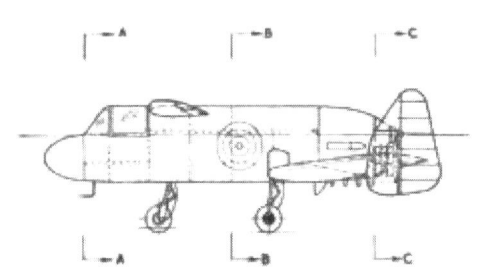

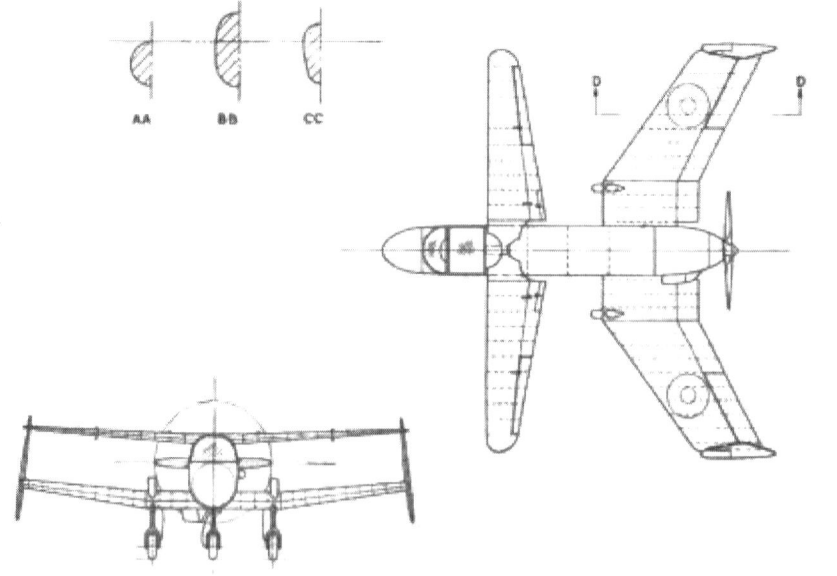

MILES M.37

Spec. T. 7 / 45.

A two seat training version of the Martinet, fitted with dual controls and a raised rear cockpit for the instructor.
Two prototypes produced - JN 275 - which flew for the first time on the 11-4-1946.
The second prototype - JN 668 / G-AKOS
Powered by 870 h.p. Bristol Mercury 30 engine.

Performance
Maximum speed in a dive. 370 m.p.h.
Range. 370 miles.
Duration. 2 hrs. 45 mins.
Fuel capacity. 70 gallons.
Oil   "   7   "

Dimensions
Span. 39 ft. - Length. 30 ft. 11 ins.
Wing area. 242 sq. ft.

Weights
Empty. 4,511 lbs. - Loaded. 5,600 lbs.

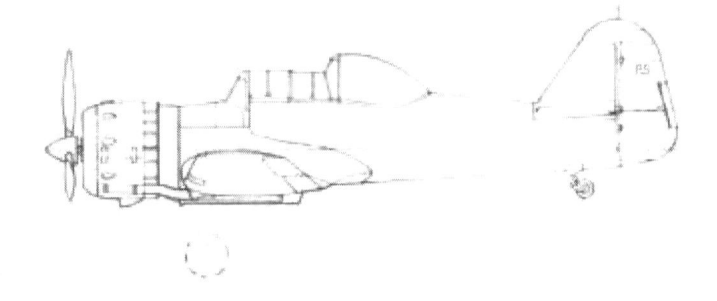

MILES M.38 MESSENGER

Spec. 17 / 43.

A development of the M.28. Mercury, as an air observation post.
A four seat light liaison and communications aircraft, for the Army.
Of a wooden construction with a plastic bonded plywood skin, also fitted with a fixed undercarriage.
The prototype - U-0223 - flew for the first time on the 12-9-1942.
Powered by De Havilland Gipsy Major engine.
Three types of tail fins were trialled, the triple proving to be the most satisfactory.
Due to interdepartmental posturing in the Ministry, the Army never got the aircraft they urgently required in quantity.

Mk. I - Powered by 145 h.p. Gipsy Major ID engines.
Nos. RH 368 to RH 378 - RH 420 to RH 429 - Served with the R.A.F. some were later sold to the Civil market and were known as Messenger **Mk.IV.A**'s.
These were the ex-R.A.F. Mk.I's converted to Mk.IV'As for civilian use, of which there were nineteen :-
Nos. 4691 / RG 327 / G-ALBE - RH 368 / G-ALAP - RH 369 / G-AKZU / F-BGOM - RH 370 / G-AJDF -
RH 371 / G-ALAR / VP-KJL - RH 372 / G-AKZC - RH 376 / G-ALBP / VH-WYN - RH 377 / G-ALAH -
RH 378 / G-ALBR - RH 420 / G-2-1 / G-ALAC - RH 421 / G-ALAE - RH 422 / G-ALAG / F-BGQZ / G-ALAG -
RH 423 / G-ALAI - RH 424 / G-AKZX - RH 425 / G-ALAF / ZK-BED - 6351 / RH 426 / G-ALAW -
RH 427 / G-AKVZ - RH 428 / G-ALAV - RH 429 / G-ALAJ.

Mk. II A - Specifically built for the civil market, with a crew of one to three passengers.
Powered by 150 h.p. Blackburn Cirrus Major III engine and fitted with an oval side window, instead of square one.
Nos. 6331 / G-AGUW - 6333 / G-AHXR / YI-HRH / G-AHXR - 6334 / G-AHZT - 6335 / G-AHUI -
6336 / G-AIBD - 6337 / G-AHZU - 6338 / G-AIAJ / EI-AHL / G-AIAJ - 6339 / G-AIEK -
6340 / G-AIDH / VH-ALN - 6341 / G-AILL - 6342 / OO-CCN / VR-TAX / VP-KHG / OO-CHS / 9Q-CHS -
6344 / CC-ECA - 6345 / CC-ECB / LV-RUJ - 6346 / G-AISL - 6347 / G-AJDM - 6349 / G-AJFC -
6355 / G-AIDK - 6358 / G-AJKL - 6359 / G-AJEY - 6360 / G-AJEZ / EC-EAL / EC-ACU - 6361 / LV-RNL -
6362 / G-AILI - 6363 / G-AJFG / EI-ADT / G-AJFG - 6365 / G-AJFH - 6366 / G-AJKK - 6367 / G-AJOE -
6368 / ZS-AVY - 6369 / G-AKKC - 6370 / G-AJOC - 6371 / G-AJVC - 6372 / G-AJVL / VH-BJM -
6373 / G-AJKG / VH-AVQ - 6374 / G-AKAV - 6375 / G-AKAH / PH-NDR - 6376 / G-AKAI / VH-AVD -
6377 / G-AKBN / EI-AFM / G-AKBN - 6378 / G-AKBO - 6379 / G-AJKT - 6698 / G-AJOD -
6699 / G-AJWB - 6701 / G-AKBL / EI-AFH / G-AKBL - 6702 / G-AKAN / F-BGPU -
6703 / G-AKAO / SE-BYY - 6704 / G-AKBM - 6705 / G-AKCN / ZK-AUM - 6706 / G-AKDF -
6707 / G-AKEZ - 6708 / OO-SIX / CN-TTL - 6709 / G-AKKN - 6711 / SU-AGQ / SU-AGT -
6712 / G-AKKK / F-DADU / F-FFOU - 6713 / G-AKKI - 6714 / G-AKKM - 6715 / SU-AGP -
6716 / G-AKKO - 6717 / G-AKKL / ZK-AWE - 6723 / EP-ACE - 6724 / G-AKIM - 6725 / G-AKIS -
6726 / G-AKIR - 6727 / G-AKIP / HB-EEC - 6728 / G-AKIN - 6729 / G-AKIO / PH-NIR / G-AKIO.
G-AILI - was temporarily fitted with a Praga E flat six horizontally opposed engine, during July 1947.

Mk. II B - One Mk. II A, as a three seater - 6266 / G-AGPX.

Mk. II C - Powered by 145 h.p. De Havilland Gipsy Major ID engine - 6267 / G-AGUW / OO-CCM - with an oval rear window.

M. III - *See M. 48.*

Mk. IV - Powered by 145 h.p. De Havilland Gipsy Major ID engine.
Nos. 6330 / G-AHGE - 6332 / G-AHFP / EI-AGB - 6343 / G-AIRY / ZK-ATT - 6700 / HB-EEC / G-AKKG.

Mk. IV - IV B - Powered by 145 h.p. De Havilland Gipsy Major X engine.
Nos. 6330 / G-AHGE - 6343 / G-AIRY / ZK-ATT - 6700 / HB-EEC / G-AKKG all Mk.IV's.

Mk. V - Powered by 180 h.p. Blackburn Bombardier 702 engine, originally a Messenger Mk.I - RH 420 - was used as an engine test bed by Blackburn & General Aircraft Ltd. - G-2-1 later G-ALAC.

MILES M. 38 MESSENGER

Miles M. 48 - During 1944, one aircraft - 4690 / U-0247 / G-AGOY / HB-EIP / G-AGOY / EI-AGE - was re-engined with 150 h.p. Blackburn Cirrus Major engine and fitted with retractable flaps, plus dual controls. It was later re-designated - **Messenger M. 38 Mk.III** - but the type was not put into production.
Of the eighty one aircraft produced, fifty eight aircraft had been sold to the British market.
The type were priced at £ 2,500 = and production ceased in January 1948.

Performance
Maximum speed. 116 m.p.h. I - 135 m.p.h. II A / II B / III - 116 m.p.h. II C / IV / IVA.
Cruising " 95 m.p.h. I - 120 m.p.h. II A / II B / III - 100 m.p.h. II C / IV / IVA.
Climb rate. 660 ft./min. I - 850 ft./min. II A / II B / III - 1,100 ft./min. II C / IV / IVA.
" " to 10,000 ft. 30 mins. I - 19 mins. 30 secs.
Service ceiling. 14,000 ft. I - 16,000 ft. II A / II B / III - 17,000 ft. II C / IV / IVA.
Range. 260 miles I.
" cruising at 112 m.p.h. 460 miles. civil.
Duration. 3 hrs. 30 mins. I - 5 hrs. 15 mins. civil.

Dimensions
Span. 36 ft. 2 ins. - Length. 24 ft. - Height. 7 ft. 6 ins. - Wing area. 191 sq. ft.

Weights
Empty. 1,518 lbs. I - 1,450 lbs. II A / II B / III - 1,360 lbs. II C / IV / IVA.
Loaded. 1,900 lbs. I - 2,400 lbs. civil.

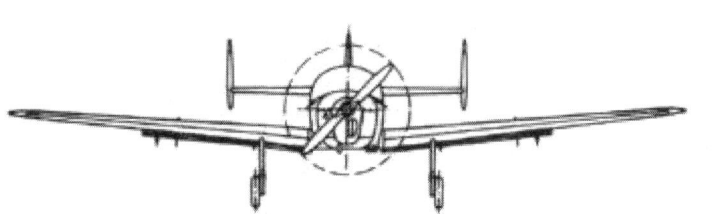

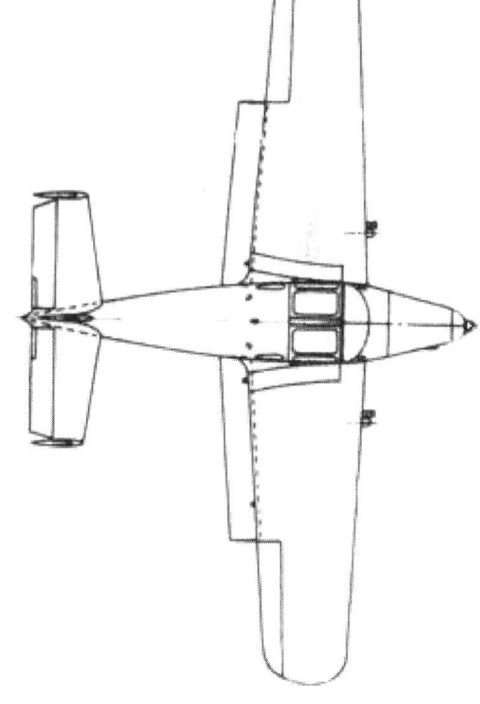

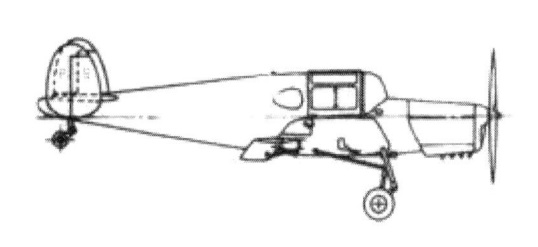

MILES   LIBELLULA   M. 39 B

M. 39 B - A two seat tandem wing research aircraft.
Of a wooden construction, with plywood and fabric covering.
Both sets of wings have ailerons and flaps, also the undercarriage is retractable.
A scale 5/8 in. model was built as a private venture - U-0244 / SR 392 / U 4 - and flew for the first time on the 22-7-1943.
Powered by two 130 h.p. De Havilland Gipsy Major I C four cylinder inverted in line air cooled tractor engines. But after two accidents and major repairs, plus all details being supplied to the U.S.A., it was returned to Miles from the Ministry and eventually scrapped some years later.

Performance
Maximum speed. 164 m.p.h.
Stalling   "   59 m.p.h.
Climb rate. 1,100 ft./min.
Fuel capacity. 25 gallons.
Oil   "   3   "

Dimensions
Span. 25 ft. front wing - 37 ft. 6 ins. rear wing.
Length. 22 ft. 2 ins. - Height. 9 ft. 3 ins.
Wing area. 61.7 sq. ft. front. -
   "   "   187.5 sq. ft. rear -
   "   "   249.2 sq. ft. total.

Weights
Empty. 2,405 lbs. - Loaded. 2,800 lbs.

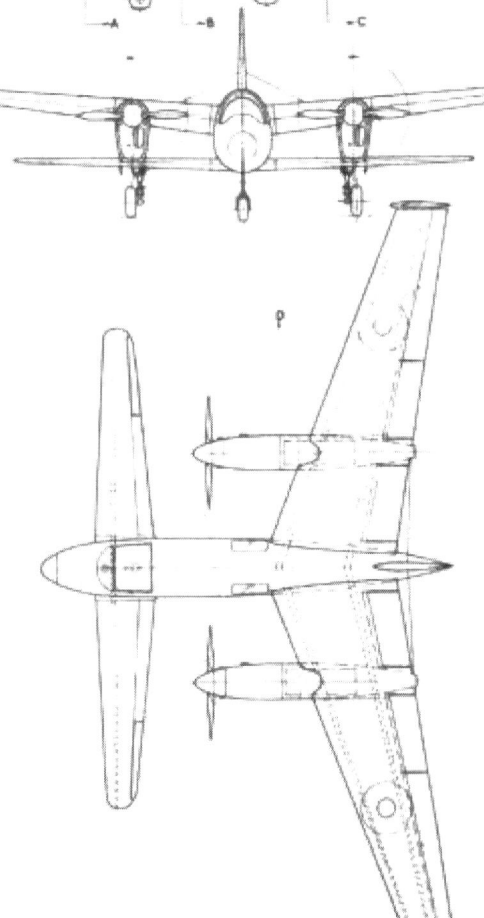

Early engine installation

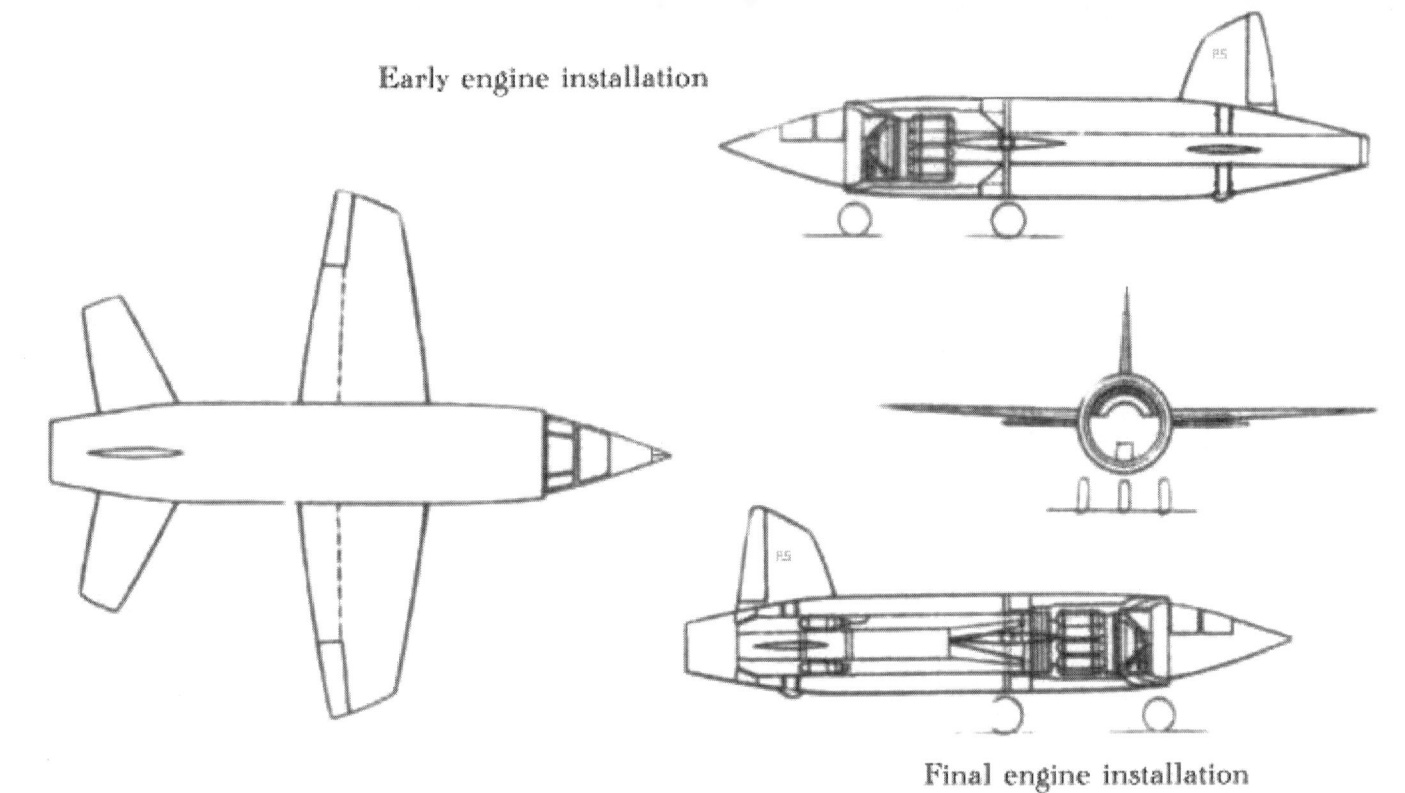

Final engine installation

MILES M.52

E.24/43

Research aircraft - (RT 133 and RT 136 issued) - Three prototypes were ordered.
Work began on the M.52 in 1943 and was cancelled in February 1946, after 90% of the work had been completed.
Powered by 2,000 lb.s.t. Power Jets W. 2 / 700 turbojet engine for sub-sonic flight, after which a ducted fan would take more air and supply a stepped up airflow approaching Mach 1, after which 4,100 lb. afterburners would be applied.
An improved version with an engine by Rolls-Royce with 6,500 lb.s.t. the A.J.65 - Avon was also proposed.
A rocket powered version was also under consideration.
The fuel was carried in an annular tank in the fuselage, surrounding the engine which was amidships.
Fitted with an all moving tailplane and a detachable cockpit pod assembly, for the pilots safety.
In the event of the aircraft failing, the pilot in his nose pod would be fired away from the rest of the fuselage. The pod would then continue groundwards supported by its own parachute and the pilot would then leave the capsule descending on his own parachute.
This being the main reason supposedly for the cancellation of the project - The pilots safety
(Pilots safety ?? Test pilots put their lives at risk every time they fly an untried aircraft, thats the job they have chosen to do).
Cancelled by Sir Ben Lockspeiser the chief scientist of the Ministry of Supply and the government of the day.
Another reason could have been that captured German documentation suggested swept wings were essential for supersonic flight.
Anyway it is now a well known fact that the cancellation of this aircraft, handed the achievements, knowledge and benefits to the Bell X I and America, who managed to achieve the required additional 20 m.p.h. over the Douglas Skystreak to obtain the record.
(Just a small thought, the Skystreak took off from the ground and the X 1 already had altitude being carried aloft and it was also dropped, without swept wings.)
It was proven some three years later by Vickers, that this aircraft would have achieved what it was meant to do.
But once again Britain lost out.

Performance - *projected*
Maximum speed. 1,000 m.p.h.
Stalling " 170 m.p.h.
Climb rate to 36,500 ft. 1 min. 30 secs.

Dimensions
Span. 26 ft. 10 1/2 ins.
Length. 33 ft. 6 1/4 ins.
Wing area. 143 sq. ft.

Weights
Loaded. 8,200 lbs.

MILES M.57 AEROVAN

A light twin engined short haul transport aircraft, designed during 1944.
Capable of carrying up to ten passengers or a ton of freight, in a 530 cubic ft. fuselage.
The fuselage is of an all wooden construction which is plywood covered, plastic bonded, with an all metal tail boom.
The wings are of an aluminium alloy single spar structure and the tail unit is of all wood, plywood covered.
Powered by two 150 h.p. Blackburn Cirrus Major III four cylinder in line inverted air cooled engines, with fixed pitch propellers.
The standard Aerovan has a crew of two, with access to the cockpit and cabin was through a door in the forward fuselage on the starboard side.
As a freighter with a freight cabin having a volume of 530 cubic ft. and with the rear loading doors.
The aircraft could also be fitted to be used as an ambulance, if required.

Mk. I - Prototype - 4700 / U-0248 / G-AGOZ - flew for the first time on the 26-1-1945.
Mk. II - Prototype - 6432 / U-8 / G-AGWO - which flew in March 1946, fitted out for ten passengers.
Fitted with five round windows instead of the four square ones.
Mk. III - The first production type, round fuselage windows as standard and a heavy duty rear door lock.
Nos. 6380 / G-AHTX - 6381 / OO-HOM - 6382 / G-AHXH / PH-EAB - 6383 / G-AIDI - 6384 / G-AIHK - 6385 / G-AIHL - 6386 / G-AIIG / I-VALF.
Seven built
Mk. IV - Thirty nine of the type were built, with four oval windows and various modifications.
Nos. 6387 / G-AIDJ / VP-YGL - 6388 / G-AIHJ / F-BENO - 6389 / G-AIKV - 6390 / C-602 / HK-602-P - 6391 / G-AILB / EC-EAK / EC-ACP - 6392 / G-AILC / EC-ABA - 6393 / G-AILD - 6394 / G-AILE / EC-ACQ - 6395 / G-AISE - 6396 / G-AISF - 6397 / G-AISI / OO-MAR - 6398 / G-AILM / SX-DBA - 6399 / G-AKHF / I-VALK - 6400 / G-AILF - 6401 / G-AJKP - 6402 / G-AJKM - 6403 / G-AJOF, later converted to H.D.M.105 - 6405 / G-AISG - 6406 / G-AJKJ - 6407 / G-AJKU - 6408 / G-AJKO / VP-KEN - 6409 / G-AJOB - 6410 / G-AJOG / OO-ERY - 6411 / G-AJOI - 6412 / G-AJWD - 6413 / G-AJZG / I-VALT - 6414 / G-AJTC - 6415 / G-AJTD - 6416 / G-AJTK - 6417 / G-AJWK / YI-ABV - 6418 / G-AJWI - 6419 / HB-AAA - 6420 / G-AJZN - 6421 / G-AJZP / F-OACN - 6422 / G-AJZR / TC-VAN - 6423 / G-AKKJ / CR-LCL - 6424 / G-AKHD / F-BFPF - 6426 / YI-ABW - 6427 / G-21-4 / ZK-AWW / NZ 1752 / ZK-AWW - 6428 / G-21-3 / ZK-AWV / NZ 1751 / ZK-AWV
Mk. V - One only - 6404 / G-AISJ - powered by two 145 hp. De Havilland Gipsy Major X engines.
Mk. VI - Two of the type were built - 6403 / G-AJOF - which later became the H.D.M.105, and - 6399 / G-AKHF / I-VALK - which flew for the first time on the 17-10-1947.
Powered by two 195 hp. Avco Lycoming 0-435-A engines, which increased the top speed by 20 m.p.h. and the climb rate by 50 %.
Development as an A.O.P. and seaplane versions were considered, but were not developed.
A total of 48 were produced, priced at £ 5,500 =
M. 57 A - Powered by two 340 h.p. Armstrong Siddeley Cheetah X radial engines.
Of a wooden construction and fitted with rear loading doors.
M. 72 - A projected four engined version of the Aerovan was envisaged, the work on it was started, but it was never completed (Specs. as the M.68).

MILES M. 57 AEROVAN

Performance
Maximum speed. 130 m.p.h. I - 127 m.p.h. - 150 m.p.h. 57A.
Cruising   "   110 m.p.h. I - 112 m.p.h. - 130 m.p.h. 57A.
Climb rate. 620 ft./min. II / III / IV
   "   " to 5,000 ft. with 5,400 lb. load. 11 mins. 45 secs.
   "   "   "   "   " 5,800 lb.   "   14 mins. 50 secs.
Service ceiling. 13,250 ft. II / III / IV.
Fuel capacity. 50 gallons.
Oil   "   5   "
Range. 450 miles. I / 57A - 400 miles.
Take off run. 72 ft. empty - 705 ft. loaded.

Dimensions
Span. 50 ft. 57 - 67 ft. 6 ins. 57A.
Length. 34 ft. 4 ins. 57 - 45 ft. 57A.
Height. 13 ft. 6 ins.
Wing area. 390 sq. ft.

Weights
Empty. 3,410 lbs. I - 3,070 lbs. II
   "   5,360 lbs. 57A.
Loaded. 5,900 lbs. I - 5,800 lbs. II
   "   11,000 lbs. 57A.

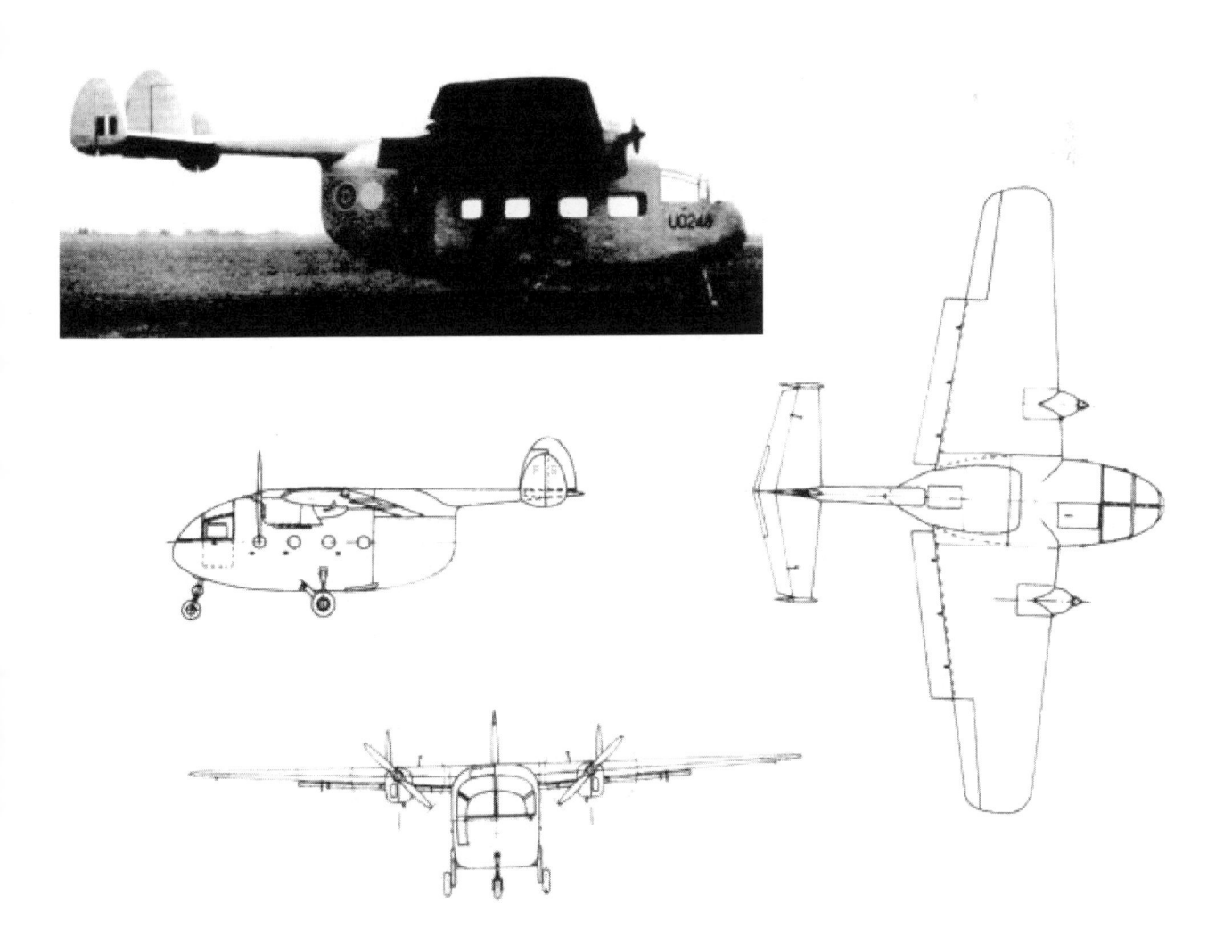

MILES M.60 MARATHON

Spec. 18 / 44.

The first four engined built by Miles and the first Miles aircraft of an all metal construction.
As a light transport high winged monoplane aircraft, originally as a private venture.
Powered by four 330 h.p. De Havilland Gipsy Queen 71 engines.
The prototype - 6265 / U-10 / G-AGPD - was flown with great satisfaction during 1946, but was lost whilst being trialled due to a fatal mistake.
A second prototype - 6430 / G-AILH / VX 229 - flown on the 27-2-1947.
The third prototype - G-AHXU - became the propeller turbine powered M. 69. Marathon Mk.II.
The cabin was 18 ft. in length, 7 ft. 9 ins. wide and just over 6 ft. high, which gave a cubic volume of 774 ft.
Due to the structure of the way aircraft were ordered / configured / constructed / paid for by this countries establishments (inter ministerial departments, who were in conflict with each other and their continued interference) the company collapsed.
The initial price for the aircraft applied for by Miles was £ 40,000 =, the Ministry offered £ 32,000 =, the production order for fifty aircraft could not be fulfilled - and so.
Handley Page was handed the contract and built forty of the type at an increased individual price for each aircraft, more than Miles had originally asked for (???)
Many of the aircraft that were built were supposed to be for B.E.A., who refused to accept them.
Due to basically a lack of communication by Ministry Departments.
Most of the aircraft were modified to serve with the R.A.F.

T. Mk. II - Nos. 101 / G-ALUB / XA 249 - 102 / G-ALVW / XA 250 - 103 / G-ALVX / XA 251 -
104 / G-ALVY / XA 252 - 105 / G-ALXR / XA 253 - 106 / G-AMAX / XA 254 - 107 / G-AMAY / XA 255 -
108 / G-AMDH / XA 256 - 109 / G-AMEK / XA 257 - 110 / G-AMEL / XA 258 - 111 / G-AMEM / XA 259 -
112 / G-AMEO / VR-NAI / D-CFSA - 113 / G-AMEP / XA 260 - 114 / G-AMER / XA 261 -
115 / G-AMET / XA 262 - 116 / G-AMEU / XA 263 - 117 / G-AMEV / XA 264 - 118 / G-AMEW / XA 265 -
119 / G-AMGN / XA 266 - 120 / G-AMGO / XA 267 - 121 / G-AMGP / XA 268 - 122 / G-AMGR / XA 269 -
123 / G-AMGS / XA 270 - 124 / G-AMGT / XA 271 - 125 / G-AMGU / XA 272 - 126 / G-AMGV / XA 273 -
127 / G-AMGW / VR-NAN - 128 / G-AMGX / VR-NAO / VK 501 - 129 / G-AMHR / VR-NAR -
130 / G-AMHS / VR-NAS / XJ 830 - 131 / G-AMHT / XA 274 - 132 / G-AMHU / XA 275 -
133 / G-AMHV / VR-NAT / XJ 831 - 134 / G-AMHW / VR-NAU - 135 / G-AMHX / XA 276 -
136 / G-AMHY / XA 277 / JA-6009 - 137 / G-AMHZ / XA 278 / JA-6010 - 138 / G-AMIA / XY-ACX -
139 / G-AMIB / XY-ACY - 140 / G-AMIC / XY-ACZ.

Some aircraft were exported to :- Burma, Canada, Japan, Jordan, Nigeria and West Germany.
M. 69 - MARATHON Mk. II - *Spec. 15 / 46.* - Powered by two 1,010 h.p. Armstrong Siddeley Mamba engines.
Accommodation for 18 passengers, also provision was made for the fitting of Rolls-Royce Dart engines.
The prototype - G-AHXU / VX 231 - flew on the 23-7-1949.
The aircraft was later fitted with reversible pitch propellers.
During 1955 the engines were replaced with two Alvis Leonides Major radial engines.
See also :- HANDLEY PAGE MARATHON.

Performance
Maximum speed. 200 m.p.h. 60 - 290 m.p.h. 69.
Cruising   "   175 m.p.h. 60 eco. - 260 m.p.h. 69.
Climb rate. 1,010 ft./min. 60 - 2,100 ft. 69.
   "   "   on 3. 566 ft./min. 60 - 700 ft./min. 69.
   "   "   to 10,000 ft. 5 mins. 69.
Service ceiling. 16,500 ft.
Range. 850 miles. 60 - 900 miles. 69.
Duration. 4 hrs. 30 mins. 60 - 3 hrs. 30 mins. 69.
Fuel capacity. 240 gallons. 60 - 400 gallons. 69.
Oil   "   24   "

Dimensions - Span. 65 ft. - Length. 52 ft. 1 ins. - Height. 14 ft. 1 ins. - Wing area. 498 sq.ft.
Weights - Empty. 11,460 lbs. 60 - 10,850 lbs. 69. - Loaded. 16,500 lbs. 60 - 18,000 lbs. 69.

MILES   M.64 - L.R.5

A two seat light monoplane for the club or private owner, built by employees of Miles Aircraft, during 1944 / 45.
Of a wooden construction, with a fixed tricycle undercarriage.
Powered by 100 h.p. Blackburn Cirrus Minor engine and flew for the time on the 3-6-1945.
No further development.
Dimensions - Span. 36 ft.
Weights
Empty. 1,000 lbs. - Loaded. 1,550 lbs.

G.E.C. - FERRANTI - Thermal Imaging Airbourne Laser (TIALD) ordered during the late eighties.
Became operational during 1991 and was used in the Gulf War.
Two pods were used on five aircraft (Tornado G.R.I's), but these did not contain the T.V. sensors.
The pod contains electro-optical equipment for the guidance of laser guided weapons (smart bombs).
The infra-red image is displayed in the cockpit.
The final decision and selection of the pre-selected target is ultimately made from the cockpit.
Target acquisition is made by the TI on a wide view setting, via the aircrafts navigational computer.
Once recognised the field of view is then narrowed for target recognition.
The system can also be used for reconnaissance.
On going development.

MILES M.65 GEMINI

A four seat, twin engined, cabin monoplane with re-tractable undercarriage.
Of a plastic bonded plywood construction.
The prototype - G-AGUS - flew for the first time on the 26-10-1945, with a fixed undercarriage.
Powered by two 100 h.p. Blackburn Cirrus Minor II engines.

Mk. IA - The first production / demonstrator aircraft was - G-AIDO - with the re-tractable undercarriage.
Powered by two 100 h.p. Blackburn Cirrus Minor II engines.
Mk. IA Special - Powered by two 130 h.p. Lycoming O-290-3/1 engines.
Mk. I B - One only - G-AJTG - fitted with re-tractable flaps.
Powered by two 100 h.p. Blackburn Cirrus Minor II engines.
Mk. II - The prototype - G-AGUS - fitted with retractable undercarriage.
Powered by two 125 h.p. Continental C-125-2 engines.
Mk. II A - Powered by two 145 h.p. De Havilland Gipsy Major X. Mk.I. engines.
Mk. III - Prototype - G-AKDC - powered by two 145 h.p. De Havilland Gipsy Major IC engines.
Mk. III A - Production version, powered by two 145 h.p. De Havilland Gipsy Major X Mk.I engines.
Mk. III B - G-AJTG - Powered by two 145 h.p. De Havilland Gipsy Major X Mk.I-III engines and fitted with re-tractable flaps.
Mk. III C - Powered by two 145 h.p. De Havilland Gipsy Major X Mk.II engines.
Mk. IV - One only - G-AKKE - as an ambulance version.
Powered by two 100 h.p. Blackburn Cirrus Minor II engines.
Mk. VII - Two only - G-AKHZ & G-AMGF - modified Mk. III's, with a bigger tail and increased weight.
Powered by two 145 h.p. De Havilland Gipsy Major X Mk.II. engines.
Mk. VIII - as the Mk.VII, but powered by two 155 h.p. Blackburn Cirrus Major III. engines.

Performance
Maximum speed 140 m.p.h. I - 145 m.p.h. IA.
Cruising   " 125 to 135 m.p.h.
Climb rate. 580 ft./min. I - 650 ft./min. IA.
   "   " to 10,000 ft. 30 mins.
Service ceiling. 13,500 ft.
Range. 750 to 1,000 miles.
Duration. 8 hrs. 15 mins.

Dimensions
Span. 36 ft. 2 ins. - Length. 22 ft. 3 ins.
Height. 7 ft. 6 ins. - Wing area. 191 sq. ft.

Weights
Empty. 1,896 lbs. I - 1,910 lbs. IA.
Loaded. 3,000 lbs. I - 3,300 lbs. III - 3,500 lbs. VII / VIII

A total of 170 Gemini's were produced, priced at £ 3,500 = and many of the type were exported.
With engine changes and various modifications the type were used in many duties, taxing, joy riding, sporting, commercial use and as ambulances, to name but a few.

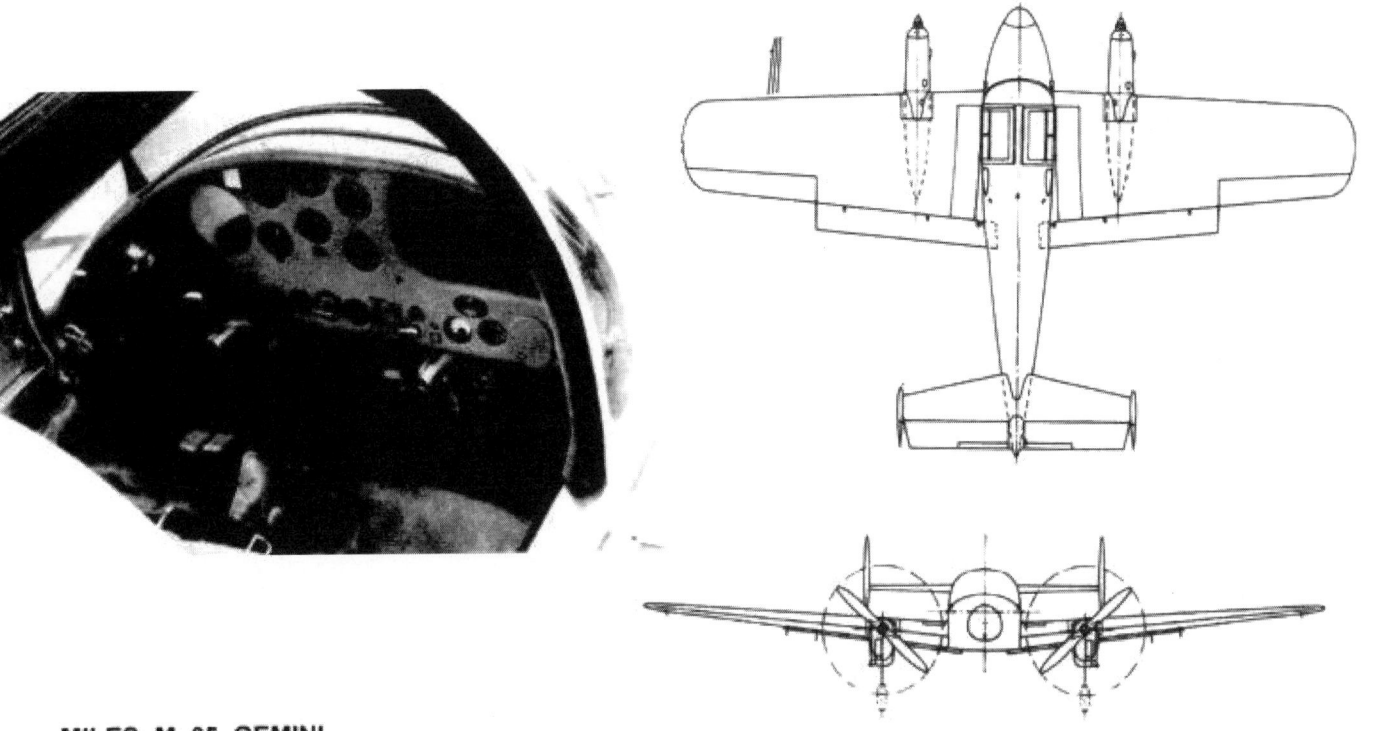

MILES M.65 GEMINI

Nos. 4701 / G-AGUS / SE-BUY - 6280 / G-AJOJ - 6281 / G-AJOK / HB-EEE / F-BEJY -
6282 / G-AJOM / PT-AHT - 6283 / G-AIHI / F-BENP - 6284 / G-AKDD -
6285 / G-AISD / VP-KDH / OO-RLD - 6286 / G-AJKN / EC-ACR - 6287 / G-AJFA / EC-ACT -
6288 / G-AJFB / EC-ACS - 6289 / G-AJKS - 6290 / G-AJWA - 6291 / G-AJWF / EI-AGF / G-AJWF -
6292 / G-AJWG - 6293 / G-AJWH / F-BJEP - 6294 / G-AKDB - 6295 / G-AJWC -
6296 / G-AKDA / SE-AYM - 6297 / G-AJZS - 6298 / G-AKDE / VP-TBI - 6299 / G-AKEG -
6300 / G-AKDL / ZK-AUA - 6301 / ZS-BRV - 6302 / G-AJTE / VP-KEG -
6303 / G-AJTF / ZS-BSP / OO-CDJ - 6304 / G-AJTH / VP-UAY / VP-KFL / G-AJTH - 6305 / G-AHKL -
6306 / G-AIDO / SE-BUG - 6307 / G-AHIM - 6308 / G-AIDG - 6309 / G-AIKW - 6310 / G-AIIE / F-BFPP -
6311 / G-AILG / F-BGPR - 6312 / G-AIIF - 6313 / VR-GGG / VR-SDJ / G-AMRG / HB-EEH -
6314 / VR-DCA - 6315 / G-AIRS - 6316 / LV-??? - 6317 / G-AKKE / CR-LCD - 6318 / LV-RGH -
6319 / G-AISK / F-BFVH / F-BFXH - 6320 / EI-ACM / G-ALUG - 6321 / G-AJOL - 6322 / ZK-ANT -
6323 / G-AISN / F-BDJD - 6324 / G-AJEX - 6325 / G-AJFD - 6326 . G-AISO / VH-AAS / VH-BJP -
6327 / G-AIWS - 6328 / G-AJKV - 6329 / G-AJTA / HB-EEA - 6444 / G-AJTI / OO-CDO -
6445 / G-AJTJ / OO-CDW - 6446 / G-AJZO - 6447 / G-AKES / YV-P-AED - 6448 / G-AKDJ -
6449 / G-AKDH / VH-AJW / VH-AJC - 6450 / G-AKDG / F-BBSL - 6451 / G-AKDI / F-BGTM -
6452 / G-AJWE - 6453 / G-AILK / VH-BJZ - 6454 / G-AISM - 6455 / G-AJKR / I-AJKR -
6456 / G-AJOH / CF-HVK - 6457 / G-AJTB - 6458 / HB-EKS - 6459 / G-AJTG -
6460 / G-AJWL / OO-ODR - 6461 / G-AJTL - 6462 / G-AJZI - 6463 / VP-RAU / VP-YLJ - 6464 / YI-ABC -
6465 / G-AJZJ - 6466 / G-AJZK - 6467G-AJZL / VH-ALJ - 6468 / G-AJZM / VH-BLN - 6469 / G-AKDK -
6470 / G-AKEI / EI-AHN / G-AKEI - 6471 / ZK-ANU - 6472 / ZK-AQO -
6473 / G-AKEH / VR-SDC / VH-ALP - 6474 / G-AKGA / OO-CMA - 6475 / F-BDAJ -
6476 / G-AKFZ / OO-CDX - 6477 / G-AKHR / VT-CQZ - 6478 / VP-UAZ / VP-KFJ / G-AOXW -
6479 / G-AKKH - 6480 / OO-CDP - 6481 / OO-CDV - 6482 / G-AKEJ - 6483 / G-AKEK -
6484 / G-AKEL - 6485 / G-AKEM - 6486 / G-AKEN / VH-BTP - 6487 / G-AKEO / VP-KET / G-AKEO -
6488 / G-AKGE / EI-ALM / G-AKGE - 6489 / G-AKGC - 6490 / G-AKHC - 6491 / G-AKER -
6492 / G-AKGD - 6493 / G-AKEP / 4X-ACK - 6494 / G-AKFU - 6495 / G-AKFV / VP-KEX -
6496 / U 23 / G-23-2 / G-AKDC / VR-TBP - 6497 / VH-AKV - 6498 / CR-GAD - 6499 / LV-??? -
6500 / LV-??? - 6501 / G-AKFW / VP-RBK - 6502 / G-AKFX - 6503 / G-AKFY / HB-EEF / G-AKFY -
6504 / G-AKGB / VH-BMW - 6505 / SU-ADY / SE-AYA - 6506 / SU-AEL - 6507 / G-AKHA -
6508 / G-AKHB - 6509 / G-AKHE - 6510 / G-AKHS / OO-GAR / CR-LCX - 6511 / G-AKHH / F-BFPG -
6512 / G-AKHI / SU-AGG - 6513 / G-AKHJ - 6514 / G-AKHK - 6515 / G-AKHL / F-BDAF -
6516 / G-AKHM / F-BDAG - 6517 / G-AKHN / F-BDAH - 6518 / G-AKHO / F-BDAI - 6519 / G-AKHP -
6520 / EI-ADM / G-AFLT - 6521 / G-AKHT / VH-BMT - 6522 / G-AKHU / VH-BMV / VH-WEJ -
6523 / G-AKHV - 6524 / G-AKHW - 6525 / G-AKHX / OO-RVE - 6526 / G-AKHY - 6527 / G-AKHZ -
6528 / G-AKKA / LN-TAH - 6529 - 6530 / SU-AHF - 6531 / G-AKKD / VT-CTQ -
6532 / G-AKKF / VP-KJC - 6533 - 6534 / G-ALCS - 6535 - 6536 - 6537 / G-AKKB.
1002 / G-AMDE - 1003 / G-AMGF - 1004 / G-ALMU - 1005 / G-AMKZ / SE-CMX - 1006 / G-AMME.
65/1001 / G-AMBH / OO-COA - 75/1002 / G-35-1 / G-AMDJ / VH-FAV -
75/1007 / G-AOGA / EI-ANB / G-AOGA.

MILES M.68 BOXCAR

A four engined transport aircraft, with a detachable freight compartment. (Flying containerisation ?)
Similar to the Aerovan and flew for the first time on the 22-8-1947, scrapped in 1948.
One only - 6696 / G-AJJM - with a crew of one and able to carry 1,600 lbs. of freight.
Powered by four 100 h.p. Blackburn Cirrus Minor II engines.
The container which was 4 ft. 6 ins. square and ten feet long.
It was wheeled so that it could be towed to and from it's loading area.
It could then be attached to the aircraft and flown to it's required destination, a door to door service.
Containers could be refrigerated, fitted with racks also sealed for customs (*clever idea, pity it didn't take off*).

Performance
Maximum speed. 138 m.p.h.
Cruising   "   120 m.p.h.
Climb rate. 630 ft./min.
    "   "   on three. 250 ft./min.
    "   "   to 10,000 ft. 31 mins.
Range. 610 miles.
Duration. 5 hrs. 15 mins.
Fuel capacity. 100 gallons.

Dimensions
Span. 50 ft. - Length. 36 ft.
Height. 11 ft. 10 ins. - Wing area. 390 sq. ft.

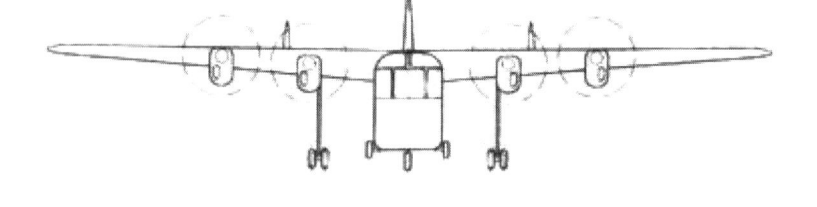

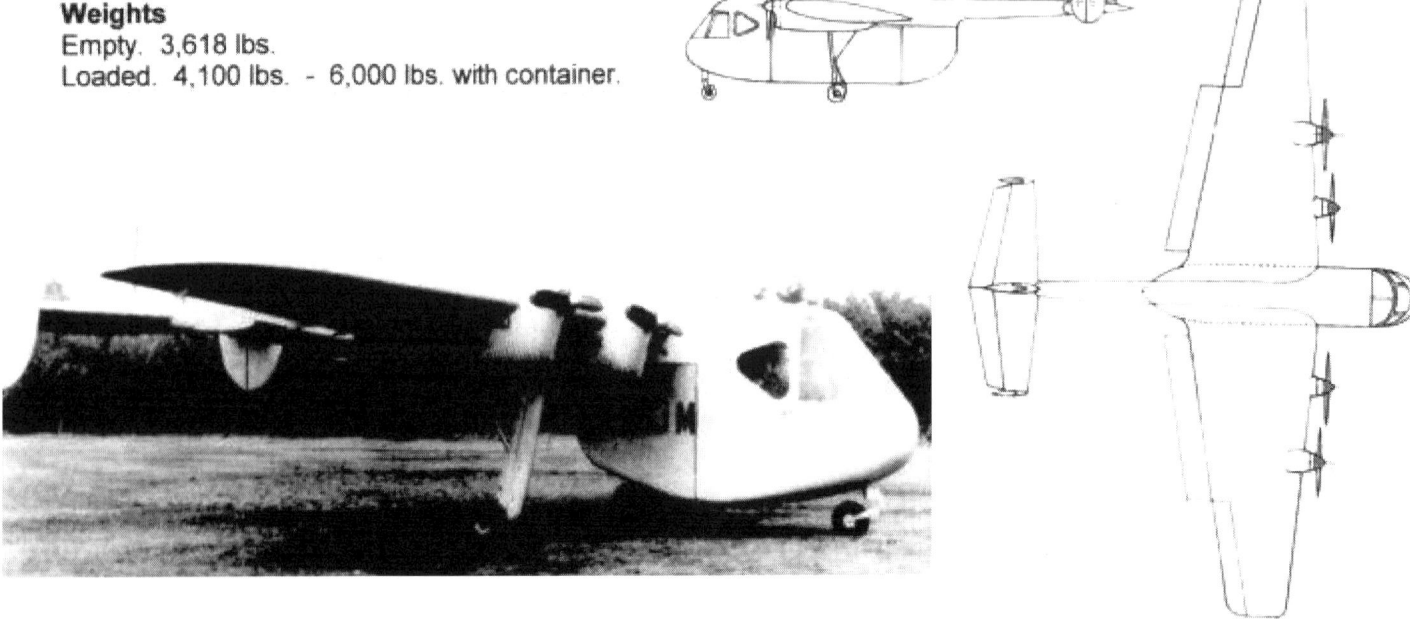

Weights
Empty. 3,618 lbs.
Loaded. 4,100 lbs. - 6,000 lbs. with container.

MILES   M.71   MERCHANTMAN

A four engined transport aircraft, with a crew of two and able to carry 2 tons of freight or twenty passengers. Similar to the Aerovan, but of an all metal construction.
One only - 6695 / U 21 / G-AILJ - flew for the first time on the 7-8-1947 and was scrapped in 1948.
Powered by four 250 h.p. De Havilland Gipsy Queen XXX engines.
The size of the cabin was 18 ft. x 7 ft. 3 ins. x 6 ft. 6 ins. with a cubic capacity of 780 ft.
A second aircraft was started upon, a box car version, but never completed due to the collapse of the company.

Performance
Maximum speed. 164 m.p.h.
Cruising   "   155 m.p.h.
Climb rate. 1,150 ft./min.
   "   "   on 3. 600 ft./min.
Range. 850 miles.

Dimensions
Span. 66 ft. 6 ins. - Length. 42 ft. 9 ins.
Wing area. 600 sq. ft.

Weights
Empty. 6,810 lbs. - Loaded. 14,000 lbs.

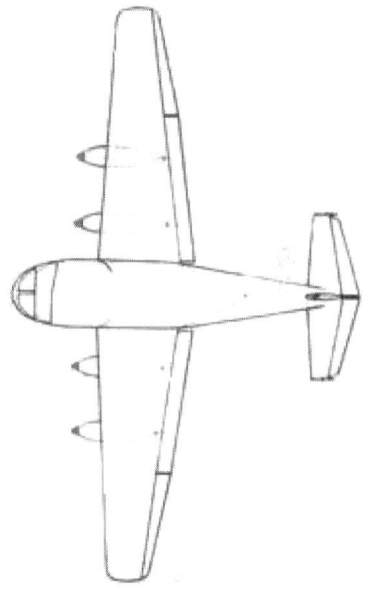

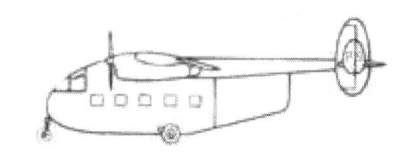

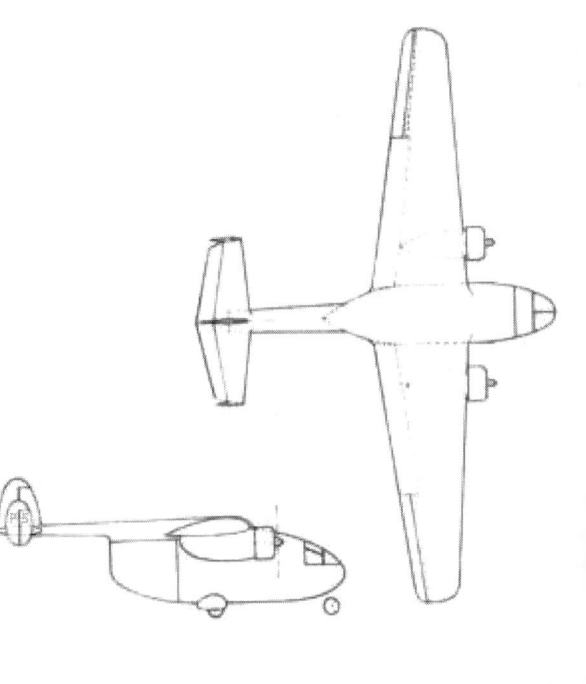

MILES   M.75   ARIES

As the M.65 Gemini, with a strengthened fuselage, larger fins and rudders.
Two only - 75/1002 / G-35-1 / G-AMDJ / VH-FAV, which flew as such in February 1951 &
105?/1009?*or 1007* / G-AOGA / EI-ANB / G-AOGA.
Powered by two 155 h.p. Blackburn Cirrus Major III engines.
Three Gemini III A's were modified to Aries standard - G-AKHZ & G-AKFX.
Powered by 145 h.p. D.H.Gipsy Major X engines and designated Gemini Mk.VII's.
The third - G-AKFX - powered by two Blackburn Cirrus Major III engines and designated Gemini Mk.VIII.

Performance
Maximum speed. 172 m.p.h.
Cruising   "   150 m.p.h.
Climb rate. 1,200 ft./min.
    "   " to 10,000 ft. 12 mins.
Service ceiling. 16,000 ft. - 20,000 ft. absolute.
Range. 675 miles. - Duration. 5 hrs. 15 mins.
Fuel capacity. 66 gallons.

Dimensions
Span. 36 ft. 2 ins. - Length. 22 ft. 3 ins.
Height. 7 ft. 6 ins. - Wing area. 191 sq. ft

Weights
Empty. 2,350 lbs. - Loaded. 3,475 lbs.

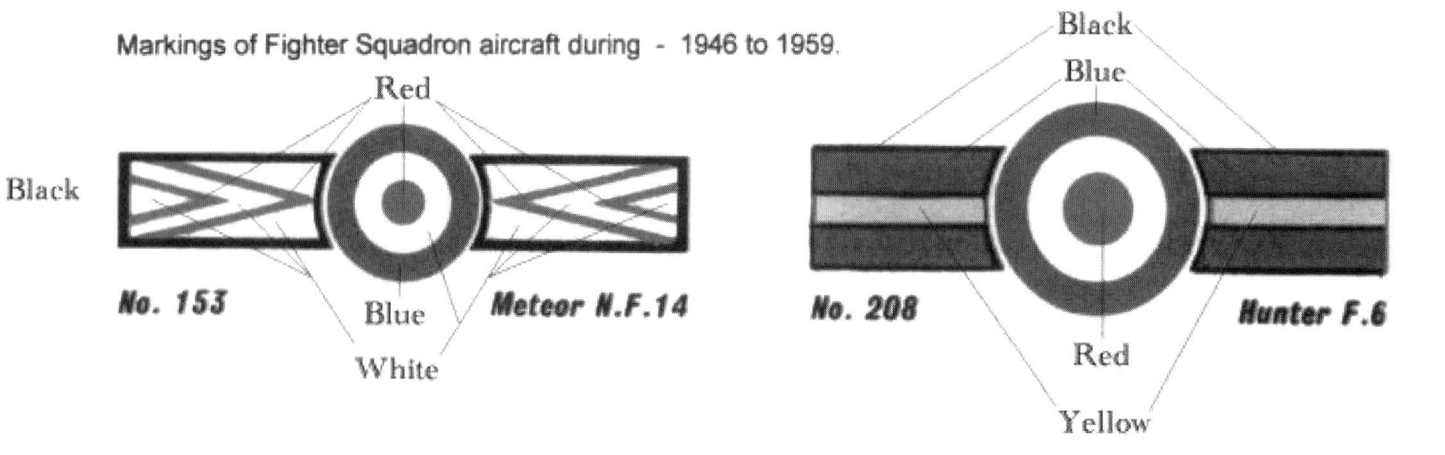

Markings of Fighter Squadron aircraft during - 1946 to 1959.

No. 153   Meteor N.F.14   (Black, Red, Blue, White)

No. 208   Hunter F.6   (Black, Blue, Red, Yellow)

MILES M.76

During 1950 / 53 F.G.Miles Ltd., had developed a method of vacuum moulding using phenolic / asbestos fibre which was stabilized with a paper honeycomb.
Using this method a wing of Durestos, made in two 30 ft. mouldings was completed.
This was intended to be fitted to the M.76 Crabpot glider and to be flown in the 1954 World Gliding Championships.
But due to some doubts about the wing, a plywood wing of the same specifications was made by Elliotts of Newbury and fitted to the aircraft.
The aircraft did not take part in the World Championships and the Durestos wing was never used.

MILES M.77 SPARROWJET

The prototype M.5 Sparrowhawk - G-ADNL - was considerably modified to a private order from its original form, during 1953.
Powered by two 330 lb.s.t. Turbomeca Palas jet engines and flew for the first time on the 14-12-1953.
The aircraft became the first jet aircraft to win the King's Cup Race in 1957, at a speed of 228 m.p.h. by Fred Dunkerley.
The aircraft was destroyed in a hangar fire in July 1964, engineless.
Performance
Maximum speed. 228 m.p.h. - Climb rate. 2,100 ft./min. - 485 ft./min. on 1 - Range. 270 miles.
Dimensions - Span. 28 ft. 6 ins. - Length. 30 ft. 9 1/2 ins. - Height. 7 ft. 2 ins. - Wing area. 156 sq. ft.
Weights - Empty. 1,578 lbs. - Loaded. 2,400 lbs.

M. 78 to M. 99 - These numbers were omitted, due to the demise of the company.
A decision was made to make a fresh start at M. 100.

MILES M.100 STUDENT

A two seat side by side basic training aircraft, which started out as a private venture by F.G. & G.Miles in 1953.
Of an all metal construction, fitted with a retractable tricycle undercarriage.
One only - 1008 / G-35-4 / G-APLK, allocated XS 941 when developed into the Mk.II version - flew for the first time on the 15-5-1957
Powered by 880 lb.s.t. Blackburn / Turbomeca Marbore II A turbojet engine.
Mk. II - Powered by Turbomeca Marbore 6F turbojet engine and flown on the 22-4-1964.
Various improvements and able to carry interchangeable underwing armament pods, for bombing training or with rockets.
Could also have been used as an air observation post or as a four seat communications aircraft which was to have been known as the 'Graduate', powered by 1,540 lb.s.t. Turbomeca Aubisque engine.
Several variants on the basic design were proposed :-
Mk. IV CENTURION - Projects, powered by 1,405 lb.s.t. Turbomeca Gourdon turbojet engine.
" V " - " " " two 550 lb.s.t. Turbomeca Arbizou turbojet engines.
Alternative engines were Armstrong Siddeley Vipers or Rolls-Royce RB.145 engines.
Also a four seat communications type, powered by two 390 lb.s.t. Blackburn Turbomeca Palas turbojet engines.
No production orders were forthcoming, other than for South Africa on which an embargo was imposed.
Not produced.

Performance
Maximum speed at sea level. 289 m.p.h.
    "   "   " 20,000 ft. 296 m.p.h.
    "   "   " 25,000 ft. 430 m.p.h. IV - 355 m.p.h. V.
Cruising   " 260 m.p.h.
Climb rate. 1,750 ft./min.
    "   " to 10,000 ft. 6 mins. 45 secs. - 3 mins. IV - 5 mins. V.
    "   "   " 20,000 ft. 17 mins. 25 secs. - 6 mins. 50 secs. IV - 12 mins. V.
Range. 450 miles.
Duration. 2 hrs. 15 mins.

Dimensions
Span. 29 ft. 2 ins.
Length. 31 ft. 6 ins.
Height. 6 ft. 3 ins.
Wing area. 144 sq. ft.

Weights
Empty. 2,400 lbs.
Loaded. 3,600 lbs.
Loaded. 3,900 lbs. with wing tanks.

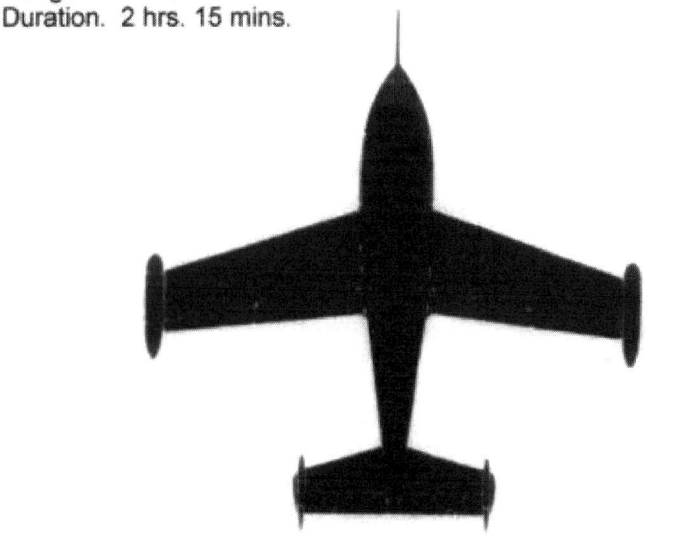

MILES H.D.M.105

Originally a Miles M.57 Mk.VI - G-AJOF - became - 105 / 1009 - G-AHDM - a twin engined experimental monoplane.
Of a wooden construction, with wings and tailboom of metal.
Powered by two 155 h.p. Blackburn Cirrus Major III engines.
Fitted with Hurel-Dubois high aspect ratio wing and flew for the first time on the 31-3-1957 as - G-35-3.
Used as a test bed for the projected larger designs :- H.D.M.106 Caravan and H.D.M.107 Aerojeep.
Damaged beyond repair in June 1958.

Performance
Maximum speed. 133 m.p.h.
Cruising   "   116 m.p.h.
Climb rate. 650 ft./min.
Service ceiling. 18,350 ft.
Fuel capacity. 26 gallons.

Dimensions
Span. 75 ft. 4 ins.
Length. 34 ft. 4 ins.
Height. 13 ft. 11 ins.
Wing area. 388 sq. ft.

Weights
Empty. 3,219 lbs.
Loaded. 6,170 lbs.

Following the success of the H.D.M.105, a new company was formed.
H.D.et M (Aviation) Ltd. - F.G.Miles Ltd., and Sociéte' de Construction des Avions Hurel-Dubios.
Projected :-
H.D.M. 106 - CARAVAN - Similar to the H.D.M. 105, but larger and as an all metal civil transport version.
Powered by two 320 h.p. Turbomeca Astazou engines or two 290 h.p. Lycoming GO-480 engines or by two 340 h.p. Lycoming GSO-480B engines.
The freight compartment was to have been 15 ft. x 6 ft. 3 ins. x 6 ft., with a cubic capacity of 563 ft.
The version was not put into production, but the design was sold to Shorts.
H.D.M. 107 - AEROJEEP - A military version of the Caravan, with S.T.O.L. capabilities as a light support type, for the U.S.Army.
Powered by two 800 s.h.p. Lycoming T-35 turboprop engines.
H.D.M. 108 - A design by Hurel-Dubios for an even larger version of the H.D.M. 106.
Specs. for 106 & 107 :-
Performance
Cruising speed. 125 to 135 m.p.h.
Climb rate. 1,560 ft./min. - 410 ft./min. on 1.
Service ceiling. 24,700 ft.
Dimensions
Span. 75 ft. 4 ins. - Length. 37 ft. 10 ins.
Height. 11 ft. 5 ins. - Wing area. 279 sq. ft.
Weights
Empty. 4,940 lbs. - Loaded. 9,500 lbs.

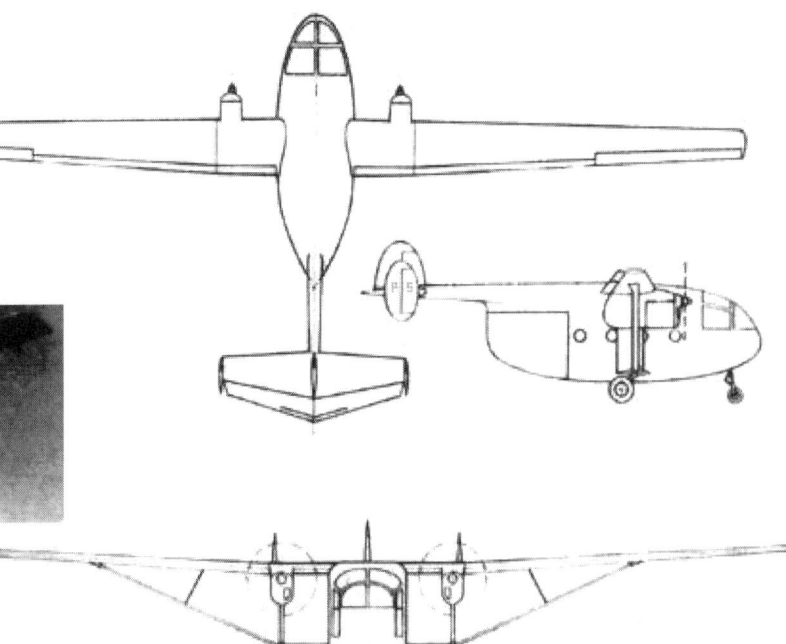

MILES   M.114 - M.218

A two / four seat light touring aircraft, fitted with a retractable tricycle undercarriage.
Of a metal and glass fibre construction.
M. 114 - Mk. I - A projected two seater, similar to the M. 74 project.
Powered by 100 h.p. Rolls-Royce Continental O-200A engine.
M. 114 - Mk. II - *later* > **M. 117** - A projected four seater version.
Powered by 145 h.p. Rolls-Royce Continental O-300A six cylinder horizontally opposed engine.
M. 115 - M. 218 - One only - G-35-6 / G-ASCK - as a four seater.
Powered by two 100 h.p. Rolls-Royce Continental O-200A engines, these were later updated to O-300A's, fitted with fully feathering constant speed propellers.
The aircraft flew for the first time on the 19-8-1962 and was to have been called the 'Martlet'.
Priced at £ 9,800 =.

Performance
Maximum speed.   123 m.p.h. 117 - 185 m.p.h. 218.
Cruising   "   115 m.p.h. 117 - 160 m.p.h. 218.
Climb rate.   825 ft./min. 117 - 1,370 ft./min. 218.
   "   "   218 on 1 - 350 ft./min.
   "   "   " to 5,000 ft. 4 mins. 218.
   "   "   "   10,000 ft. 10 mins. 218.
Service ceiling.   21,700 ft. 218.
Range.   670 miles. 117 - 1,000 miles. 218.
Fuel capacity.   30 gallons. 117 - 70 gallons. 218.
Oil   "   6   "   218.

Dimensions
Span.   37 ft.
Length.   26 ft. 1 ins. 114 - 25 ft. 4 ins. 218.
Height.   7 ft. 5 ins. - 8 ft. 6 ins. 218.
Wing area.   170 sq. ft.

Weights
Empty.   2,164 lbs. 218.
Loaded.   2,300 lbs. 114/2 - 2,750 lbs. 115.
     "   1,550 lbs. 117 - 3,200 lbs. 218.

MILES - BEAGLE M.B. 206

See :- **BEAGLE.**

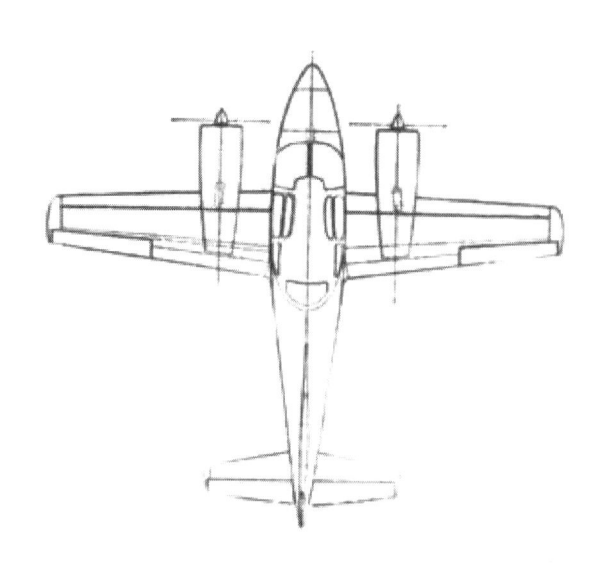

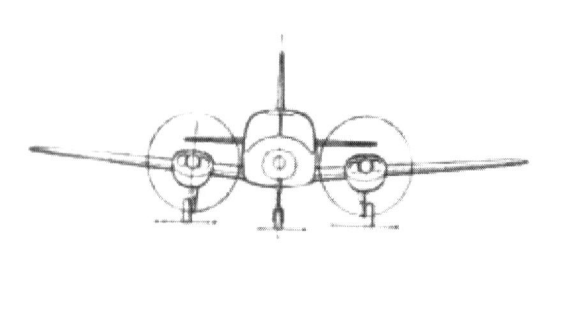

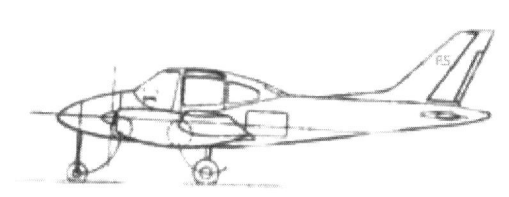

MILES PROJECTS

1933 - A design for a light training monoplane, powered by a pusher engine.

1935 - **M. 10** - *Spec. 32 / 35* - A design proposal for a radio controlled pilotless target drone. Developing the Falcon M 3B as a landplane or seaplane type.
Dimensions - Span. 35 ft. - Length. 25 ft.

1936 - *Shown below* - A projected larger version of the Peregrine and of an all metal construction, named 'Marathon'.
A four engined transport aircraft, with accommodation for 12 passengers.
Performance
Cruising speed. 184 m.p.h.
Range. 700 miles.

1940 - A project for a radio controlled pilotless aircraft 'Hoopla' - able to carry a 1,000 lb. bomb.
Directed by a radio signal to the target, probably within a few hundred yards.
A mock up was built, but the Ministry decided not to pursue the matter any further.

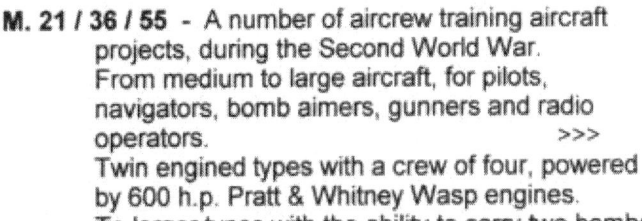

M. 21 / 36 / 55 - A number of aircrew training aircraft projects, during the Second World War. From medium to large aircraft, for pilots, navigators, bomb aimers, gunners and radio operators.
Twin engined types with a crew of four, powered by 600 h.p. Pratt & Whitney Wasp engines. To larger types with the ability to carry two bomber crews and powered by two 1,300 h.p. Rolls-Royce Merlin XX engines.

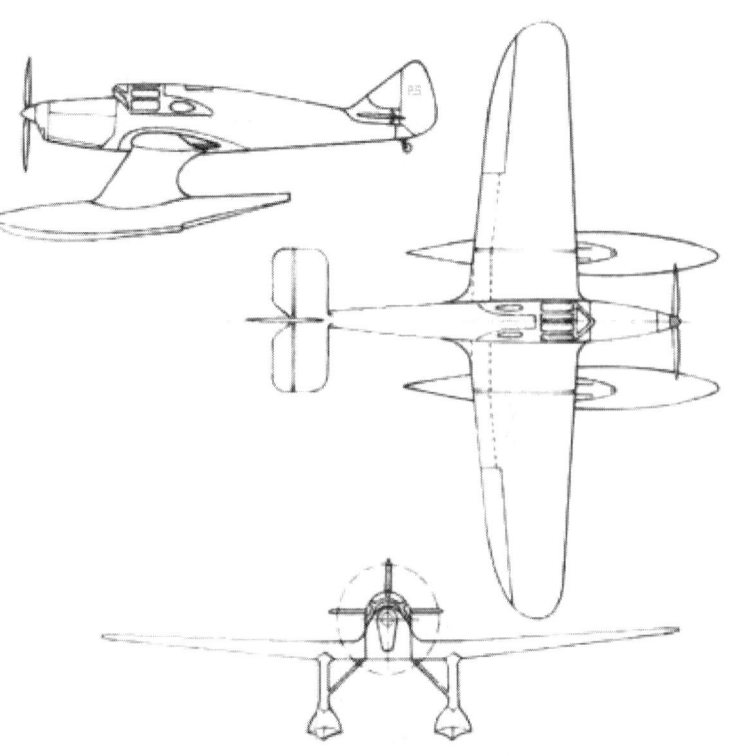

MILES PROJECTS

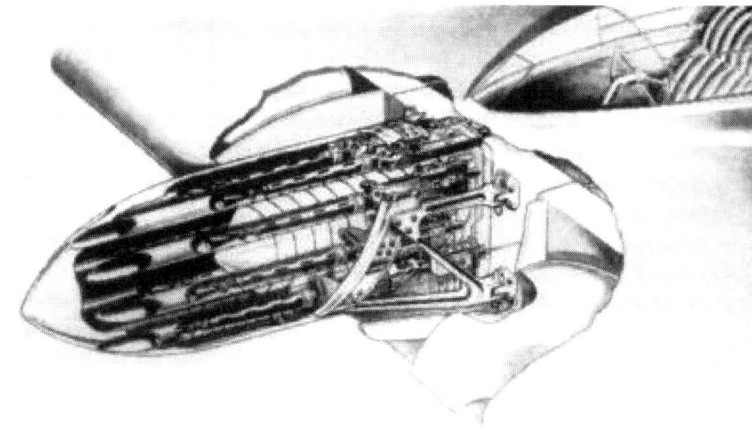

M. 22 - A project for a single seat day or night fighter aircraft.
Of a wooden construction, with metal wing spars.
Powered by two 1,600 h.p. Rolls-Royce Griffon engines.
Armed with ten 0.303 Browning machine guns in a nacelle which could be bolted to the fuselage in front of the pilots position and provided with 5,000 rounds of ammunition.
Not developed.
Performance
Maximum speed. 504 m.p.h.
Climb rate. 5,180 ft./min.
" " to 10,000 ft. 2 mins. 25 secs.
Service ceiling. 37,000 ft.
Duration. 2 hrs.
Dimensions
Span. 39 ft. - Length. 33 ft.
Height. 9 ft. - Wing area. 325 sq. ft.
Weights
Loaded. 13,000 lbs.

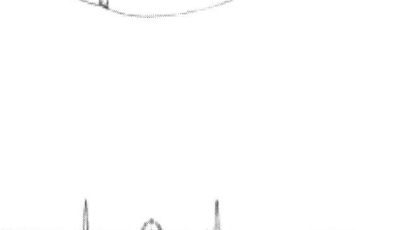

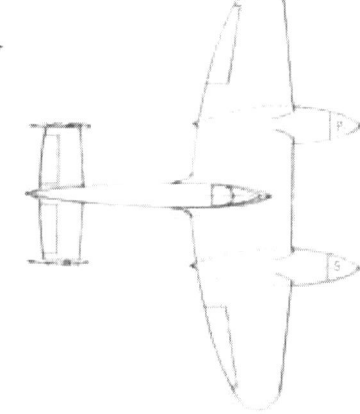

M. 22 A - *Spec. F. 18 / 40.* - A project for a tandem two seat high altitude day or night fighter aircraft.
Larger than the M.22 and armed with four 20 mm. cannon.
Of a wooden construction and with a pressurized cabin.
Powered by two Rolls-Royce Merlin 60 or XX engines.
Another projected version of the type, with a Boulton Paul four gun turret.
Not developed.
Performance
Maximum speed. 425 m.p.h. 60's - 405 m.p.h. XX's.
Absolute ceiling. 43,000 ft. 60's - 40,000 ft. XX's.
Duration. 4 hrs. normal - 6 hrs. max.
Dimensions
Span. 51 ft. - Length. 35 ft.
Height. 11 ft. 6 ins.
Wing area. 460 sq. ft.
Weights
Loaded. 16,500 lbs.

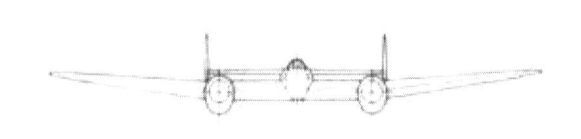

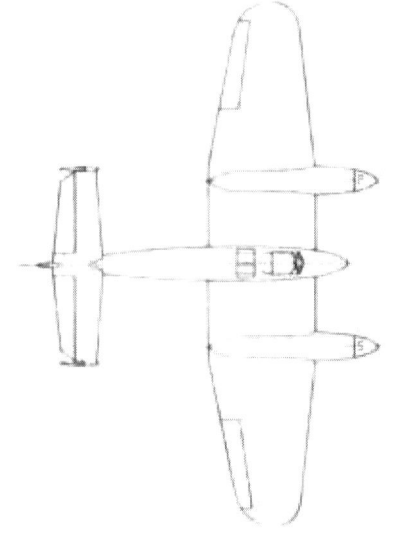

MILES PROJECTS

M. 23 - A proposal for a single seat high speed fighter.
Of a wooden construction, with metal wing spars.
Powered by a 1,075 h.p. Rolls-Royce Merlin X or 1,600 h.p. Rolls-Royce Griffon engine.
Armed with eight 0.303 Browning machine guns, with 500 rounds of ammunition for each gun or two 20 mm. Hispano cannon.
Not developed.

Performance
Maximum speed. 411 m.p.h. Merlin - 470 m.p.h. Griffon.
Climb rate. 2,770 ft./min. Merlin - 4,680 ft./min. Griffon.
  "   " to 10,000 ft. 5 mins. 15 secs. Merlin - 3 mins. Griffon.
Service ceiling. 26,000 ft. Merlin - 38,000 ft. Griffon.
Duration. 3 hrs. 15 mins. Merlin - 2 hrs. 15 mins. Griffon.

Dimensions
Span. 31 ft. - Length. 28 ft. 8 ins.
Height. 8 ft. - Wing area. 185 sq. ft.

Weights
Loaded. 6,200 lbs. Merlin
   "   7,400 lbs. Griffon.

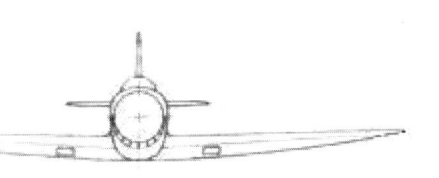

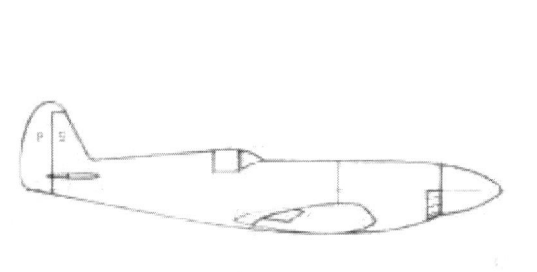

M. 23 A - A projected design for a high altitude day or night fighter aircraft.
Powered by a Rolls-Royce Merlin 60 engine.
Armed with two 20 mm. cannon, with 60 rounds of ammunition for each gun.
Fitted with cabin pressurisation and fuel drop tanks.
Not developed.

Performance
Maximum speed. 440 m.p.h.
Service ceiling. 45,000 ft.
Fuel capacity. 83 gallons norm.
Oil   "   5 1/2   "

Dimensions
Span. 50 ft. - Length. 31 ft.
Wing area. 262 sq. ft.

Weights
Empty. 6,240 lbs. - Loaded. 7,440 lbs.

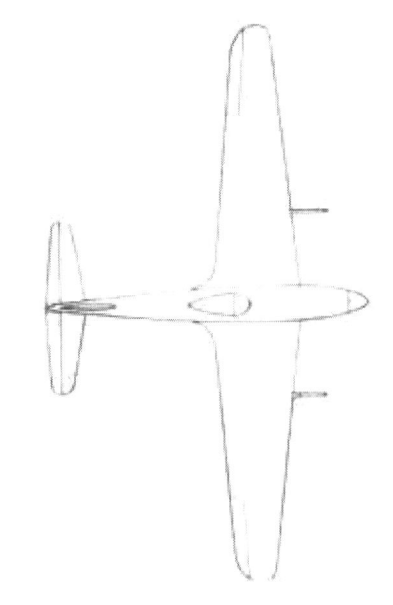

MILES PROJECTS

1942 - A design project for a Glider Tug.
A twin engined tail first aircraft, with tricycle undercarriage and of an all wooden construction.
Powered by two 870 h.p. Bristol Mercury air cooled radial engines.
Able to tow a Horsa glider for an operational range of 520 miles and returning alone.
Performance
Cruising speed. 116 m.p.h.
Fuel capacity. 417 gallons.
Oil   "   34   "
Dimensions
Span. 46 ft. - Length. 34 ft. 6 ins.
Wing area. 377 sq. ft.
Weights
Empty. 6,980 lbs.
Loaded. 11,306 lbs.

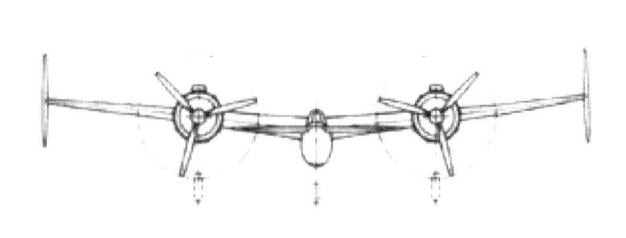

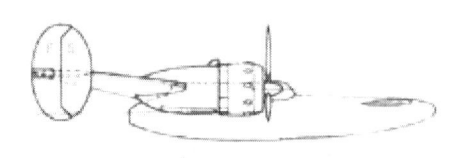

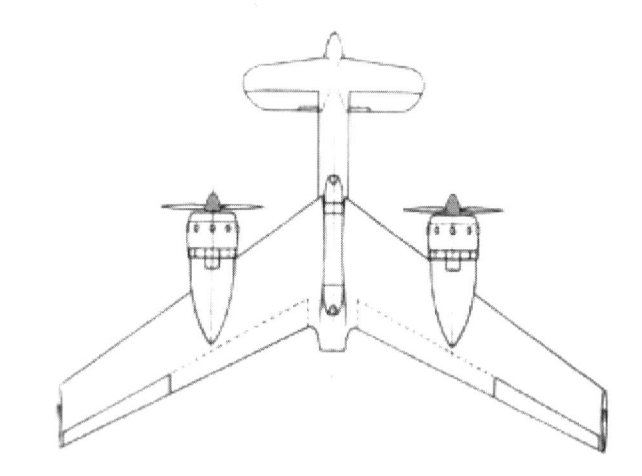

1942 - A project for the Libellula heavy bomber.
Powered by six 2,400 h.p. Bristol Centaurus 3SM sleeve valve air cooled radial engines.
Armed with ten 0.303 Browning machine guns, mounted in four turrets.
Not developed.
Performance
Maximum speed. 310 m.p.h.
Cruising   "   240 m.p.h.
Range with 37,000 lbs. of bombs. 2,000 miles.
    "   "   51,000 lbs. "   "   1,330   "
Dimensions
Span. 115 ft. - Wing area. 2,700 sq. ft.
Weights
Loaded. 150,000 lbs.
A variant was later submitted as an eight engined type, with the turrets amidships deleted.
Powered by 2,300 h.p. Rolls-Royce P.I.26 or 2,500 h.p Napier Sabre engines.

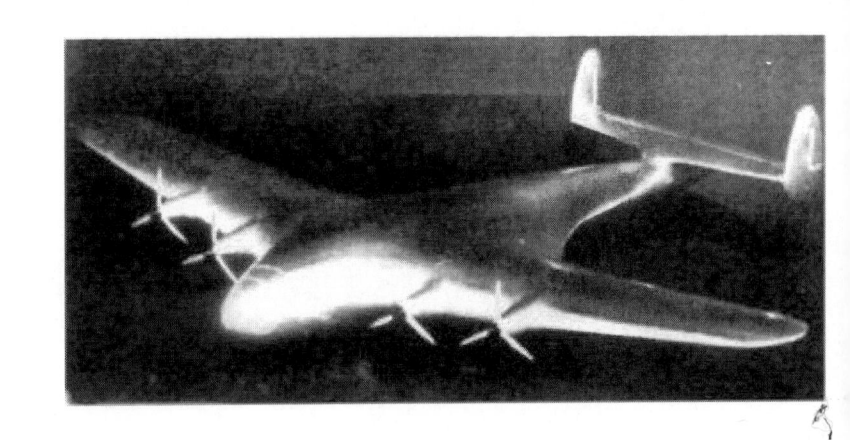

M. 26 - X Projects

1938 - Secret projects.
X 2 - A design project for a large passenger transport aircraft, with accommodation for 38 passengers.
Powered by four 900 h.p. Rolls-Royce air cooled engines.
Spec. 42/37 - A small twin engined scale model was produced.
Performance
Maximum speed. 301 m.p.h. - Cruising speed economical. 227 m.p.h. - Climb rate to 11,000 ft. 9 mins. 35 secs. - Service ceiling. 30,000 ft. - Fuel capacity up to 2,500 gallons. - Range. 4,300 miles.
Dimensions - Span. 99 ft. - Length. 78 ft. 10 ins. - Wing area. 1,762 sq. ft.
Weights - Empty. 26,983 lbs. - Loaded. 61,000 lbs.

X 3 - A six engined version of the X 2, was also envisaged, also not developed.
>>>

X 4 - X 5 - X 6 - X 8 -
Similar projects of various sizes.

1941 - X 7 - An eight engined transatlantic version.
>>>

MILES PROJECTS - M. 26

1942 - X 9 - A project for a four engined long range transport aircraft.
Of an all metal stressed skin construction, with a tricycle undercarriage.
Powered by four Rolls-Royce Griffon II engines.
Accommodation for forty seven troops plus their equipment.
Not developed.

Performance
Cruising speed. 295 m.p.h.
Range. 2,600 miles.
Fuel capacity. 3,000 gallons.
Oil   "   156   "

Dimensions
Span. 116 ft. - Length. 80 ft.
Wing area. 1,485 sq. ft.

Weights
Empty. 37,000 lbs. - Loaded. 76,000 lbs.

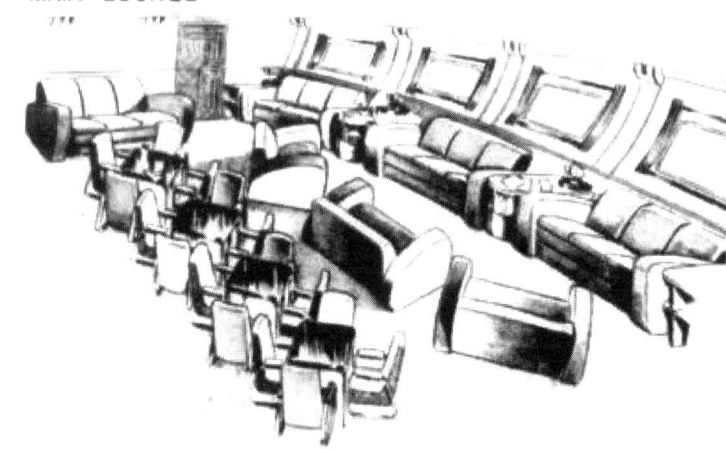

MAIN LOUNGE

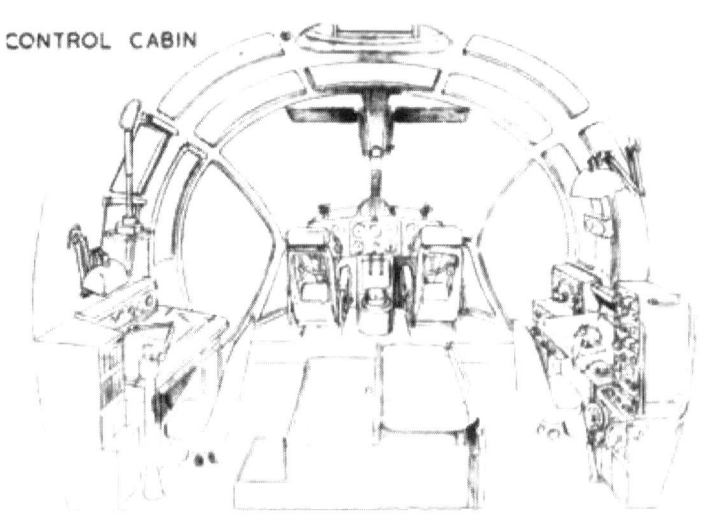

CONTROL CABIN

X 10 - A twin engined transport version.
>>>

MILES PROJECTS - M. 26

X 11 - *Private venture before Spec. 2 / 44.* - Transatlantic transport, with accommodation for fifty passengers.
Powered by eight 2,300 h.p. Rolls-Royce P.I.26 twelve cylinder engines, fitted with contra rotating propellers.

Performance
Maximum speed at 16,000 ft. 425 m.p.h.
Cruising   "   "   "   350 m.p.h.
Climb rate. 1,500 ft./min.
Range. 3,500 miles.
Fuel capacity. 7,400 gallons.
Oil   "   589   "

Dimensions
Span. 150 ft. - Length. 110 ft.
Wing area. 2,350 ft.

Weights
Empty. 75,800 lbs. - Loaded. 165,000 lbs.

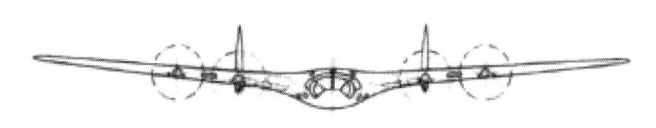

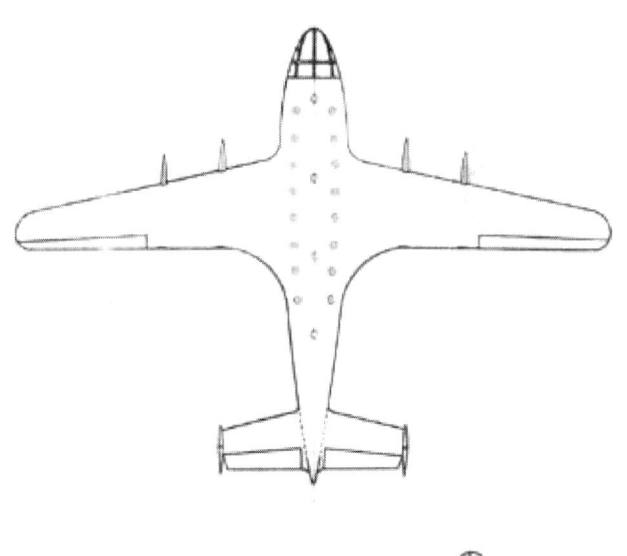

X 12 - Bomber - Short range - Medium range - Long range.
Armed with a two 20 mm. Hispano cannon in a dorsal turret and a retractable belly turret with two five inch machine guns.

Performance
Climb rate. 1,500 ft./min.
Range with 25 % fuel in reserve. 1,100 miles. s/r. - 2,200 miles. m/r. - 3,400 miles. l/r.
Dimensions - As X 11 - Bomb bay of 40 ft. in length.
Weights
Empty. 77,000 lbs. s/r. - 80,000 lbs. m/r. - 84,000 lbs. l/r.
Bomb load. 60,200 lbs. s/r. - 38,700 lbs. m/r. - 14,600 lbs. l/r.

X 13 - Troop transport which was able to carry an assortment of various loads.
Accommodation for up to 200 troops.
Dimensions - As X 11.

MILES PROJECTS - M. 26

X 14 - A design development of the X 11, as a civil transport type for Empire routes. Powered by four 2,400 h.p. Bristol Centaurus engines.
Performance
Cruising speed. 260 m.p.h.
Range. 2,600 miles.
Fuel capacity. 4,500 gallons.
Oil   "   322   "
Dimensions - As the X 11.
Weights
Empty. 58,000 lbs. - Loaded. 120,000 lbs.

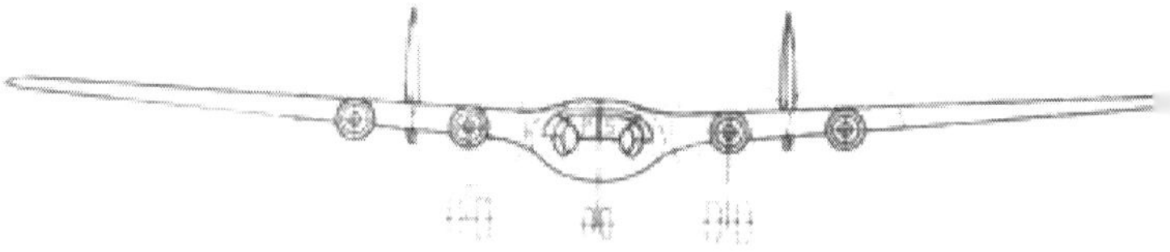

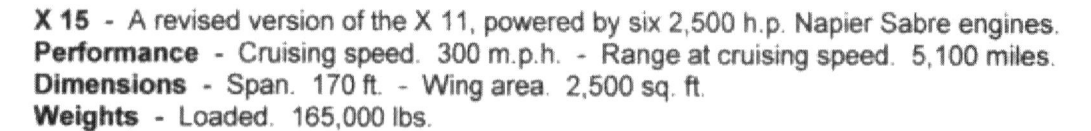

X 15 - A revised version of the X 11, powered by six 2,500 h.p. Napier Sabre engines.
Performance - Cruising speed. 300 m.p.h. - Range at cruising speed. 5,100 miles.
Dimensions - Span. 170 ft. - Wing area. 2,500 sq. ft.
Weights - Loaded. 165,000 lbs.

None of the X projects were developed and those of the powers to be who supposedly knew better, guided this country towards spending our money abroad, namely to the U.S.A.
In hindsight *(which is a beautiful thing)* the Ministry eventually reduced our aviation industry to virtually nil.

BRITISH AEROSPACE DYNAMICS ASRAAM
Advanced Short-Range Air to Air Missile, powered by a rocket motor.
To replace the Sidewinder Missile during the late 1990's.
A joint co-operation missile - Infra-red by Hughes Co. of U.S.A. - Rocket by B.Ae. Royal Ordnance Div. - Warhead by Messerschmitt-Bolkow-Blohm of Germany.
A fire and forget weapon, fired at right angles to targets against sophisticated ECM.
Dimensions - Length. 9 ft. 6 ins. - Diameter. 166 mm.
Weight - 192 lbs.

MILES PROJECTS

M. 29 - A project design based on the Miles Master, for a high speed advanced training type.
Powered by 1,600 h.p. Bristol Hercules or Wright Cyclone engines.
Later considered as a Target Tug of which a mock up was built, cancelled.

M. 31 - A project similar to the M.29, based on the Miles Master III, as a progressive development of the type.
Master IV - A re-designed cabin top with a better view for the instructor, modifications to the centre section and tailplane.

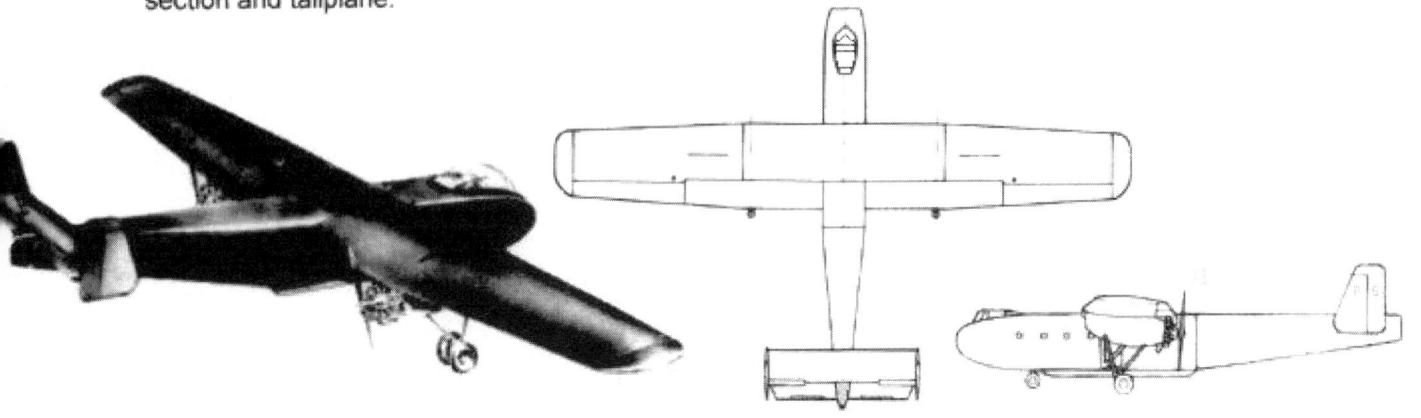

M. 32 - *Spec. X. 26/40* - A design for a high winged glider type.
Accommodation for 25 paratroops or field gun with 16 troops or 12 troops and 4 motor cycles with sidecars.
The undercarriage was to be jettisoned on take off, landing on skids.
A ramp in the nose for load access, plus doors on each side towards the rear of the fuselage.
Also as a powered glider type, with the engines in attachable nacelles.
Powered by two 800 h.p. to a 1,000 h.p. Bristol Pegasus or Mercury pusher engines.
Not developed.
Performance
Maximum speed. 185 m.p.h.
Towing   "   150 m.p.h.
Range. 1,350 miles max.
Fuel capacity. 540 gallons.
Oil   "   44   "
Dimensions
Span. 95 ft. - Length. 64 ft.
Height. 18 ft. - Wing area. 1,200 sq. ft.
Weights
Empty. 8,000 lbs. glider - 14,060 lbs. engined.
Loaded. 14,900 lbs. "   - 25,246 lbs.   "
Military load of 6,900 lbs.

MILES PROJECTS

M. 34 - A design for a twin engined long range ground attack fighter aircraft, with a crew of one or two.
Powered by two Rolls-Royce Merlin engines.
Armed with four 40 mm. cannon.
Also designed as a high speed target tug, both with retractable undercarriage.

M. 36 - A proposed design for a twin engined aircrew training type - The 'Montrose' - with a crew of six.
Of a stressed skin and wooden construction, with interchangeable undercarriage normal two wheel with tail wheel or tricycle type.
Powered by two 600 h.p. Pratt & Whitney Wasp S3H1 engines or two 870 h.p. Bristol Mercury engines.
A four engined type was also proposed, powered by four 420 h.p. Armstrong Siddeley Cheetah XV engines.
Not developed

Performance
Maximum speed. 220 m.p.h. Wasp - 240 m.p.h. Cheetah - 295 m.p.h. Mercury.
Fuel capacity. 250 gallons.
Oil   "   20   "

Dimensions
Span. 51 ft. 6 ins. - Length. 40 ft.
Height. 10 ft. 9 ins. - Wing area. 410 sq. ft.

Weights
Empty. 6,835 lbs. Wasp - 8,835 lbs. Cheetah.
Loaded. 10,847 lbs. Wasp - 12,847 lbs. Cheetah.

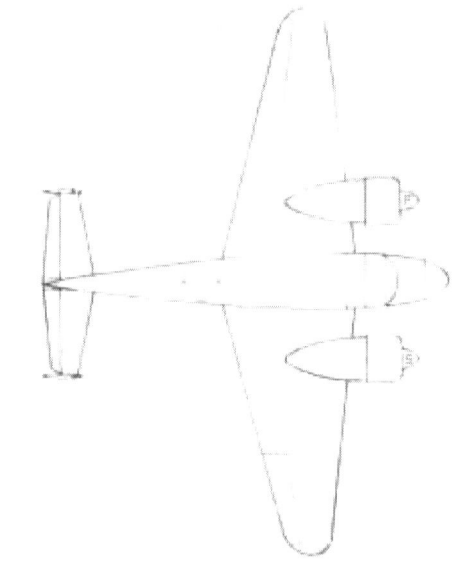

MILES PROJECTS

M. 39 - *Spec. b. 11 / 41.* - A Libellula heavy bomber project, with a crew of three, which was submitted to the Ministry during 1942.
Of an all metal construction, with a pressurised cabin and tricycle undercarriage.
Powered by initially two Rolls-Royce Merlin 60's or Bristol Hercules VIII engines or ultimately by three Power Jets W.2/500 turbojet engines.
Armed with two 20 mm. Hispano Suiza cannons in the forward wings.
Able to carry a bomb load of 7,000 lbs. or two 18 in. torpedoes.
Not developed

Performance
Cruising speed. 350 m.p.h. props.
    "   " 500 m.p.h. jets.
Range. 1,600 miles.
Fuel capacity. 585 gallons.
Oil   "   90 "

Dimensions
Span. 39 ft. 3 ins. front - 55 ft. rear.
Length. 35 ft. 9 ins.
Wing area. 139 sq. ft. front - 417 sq. ft. rear.

Weights
Empty. 12,875 lbs. - Loaded. 26,750 lbs.

M. 40 - For a large transport aircraft, of a wooden construction.
Powered by four 1,575 h.p. Bristol Hercules XI engines or four 1,600 h.p Wright Cyclone GR-2600 A5B engines.
Accommodation for up to 120 troops, the fuselage to have been fitted with front and rear loading ramps.
A six engine type was also envisaged, using the same power units as in the four engined version.

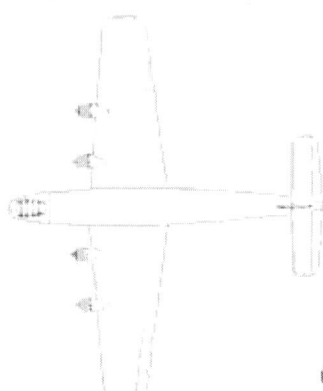

67

MILES PROJECTS

M. 41 - The six engined larger version of the M.40, with two 36 ft. x 10 ft. x 9 ft. freight compartments which gave a total of 6,480 cubic ft.
Accommodation for up to one hundred and eighty troops and both versions fitted with fixed spatted undercarriage. - Not developed.
Performance
Maximum speed. 220 m.p.h. 4.
Cruising   "   150 m.p.h. 4 - 180 m.p.h. 6.
Range. 300 miles 6.
Dimensions
Span. 112 ft. 4 - 142 ft. 6.
Length. 75 ft. 4 - 138 ft. 6.
Height. 27 ft. 6 ins. 4 - 33 ft. 6 ins. 6.
Wing area. 2,000 sq. ft. 4 - 3,360 sq. ft. 6.
Weights
Empty. 35,000 lbs. 4 - 60,000 lbs. 6.
Payload max. 28,000 lbs. 4 - 48,200 lbs. 6.
Loaded. 70,000 lbs. 4 - 117,000 lbs.

M. 42 - A proposal for a twin engined Libelulla design for a ground attack fighter type, with a variety of armaments.
Powered by two 1,600 h.p. Rolls-Royce Merlin 30 engines.
Performance - Range. 750 miles normal.
Dimensions - Span. 42 ft. 6 ins. - Wing area. 393 sq. ft.
Weights - Loaded. 14,300 lbs.

M. 43 - A single engined variant of the M. 42, powered by 2,000 h.p. Rolls-Royce Griffon engine.
Performance - Range. 750 miles normal. - **Weights** - Loaded. 11,400 lbs.
Dimensions - Span. 37 ft. - Wing area. 300 sq. ft.

>>>

M. 44 - Similar design project as the M. 34, powered by two 1,600 h.p. Rolls-Royce Merlin 30 engines.
Performance - Range. 750 miles normal.
Dimensions - Span. 48 ft. - Wing area. 425 sq. ft.
Weights - Loaded. 14,700 lbs.

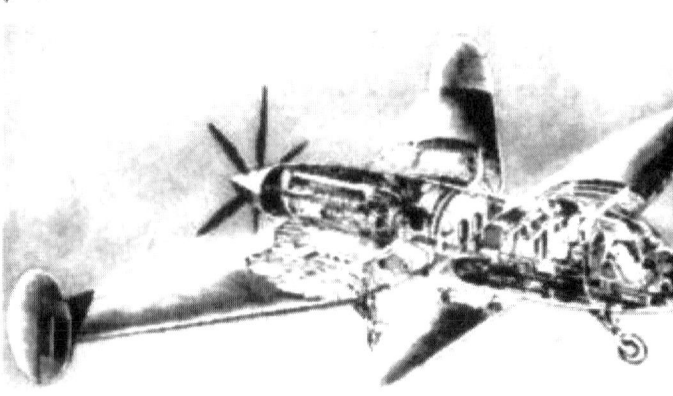

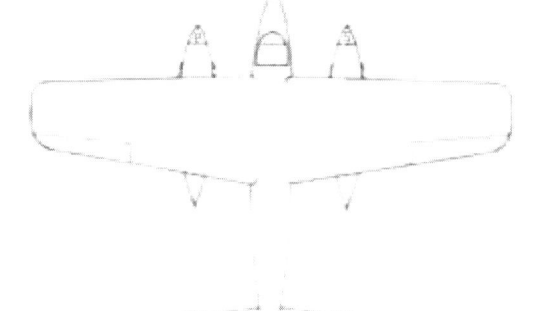

MILES PROJECTS

1943 - M. 45 - A design for a tandem two seat elementary and advanced training aircraft, combined in one type.
Powered by a 250 h.p. De Havilland Gipsy Queen 51 engine.
A mock up was built, but the project was never completed.
Performance - Est. maximum speed. 200 m.p.h. - Stalling speed. 50 m.p.h.

M. 46 - A design for an experimental engine test bed aircraft, using the wings and undercarriage of a North American Mustang.
The new fuselage was to have two seats in tandem.
Powered by 2,300 h.p. Rolls-Royce P.I.26 twelve cylinder water cooled diesel engine (Crecy).
Accepted by Rolls-Royce, rejected by the Ministry.
Abandoned.
Dimensions - Span. 40 ft. 3 ins. - Length. 32 ft. 6 ins. - Wing area. 265 sq. ft.
Weights - Empty. 5,430 lbs. - Loaded. 8,360 lbs.

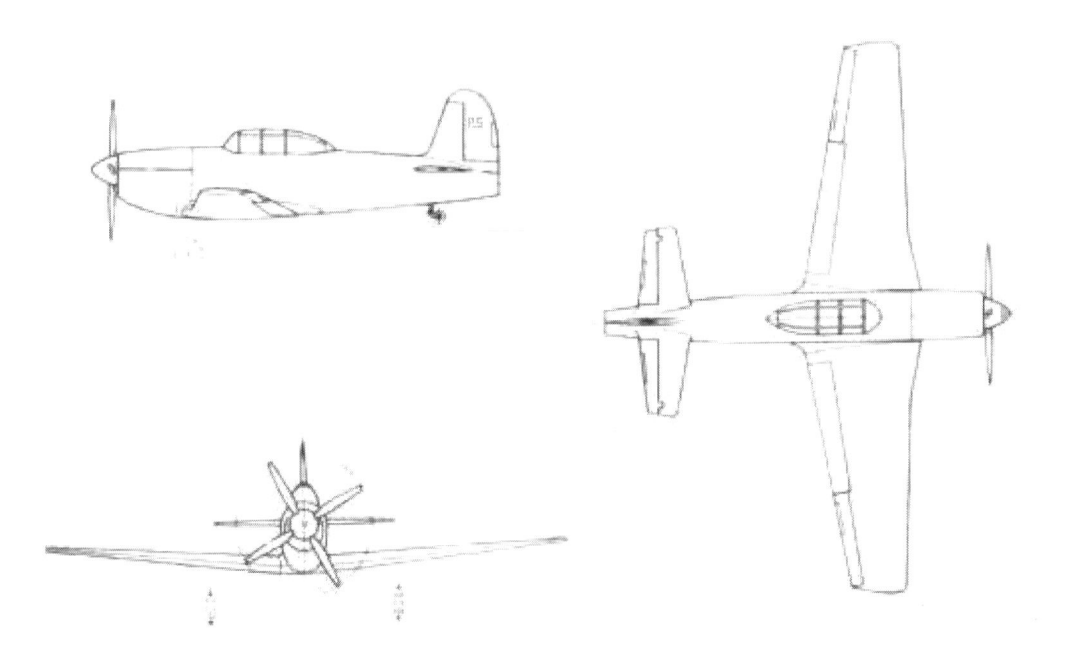

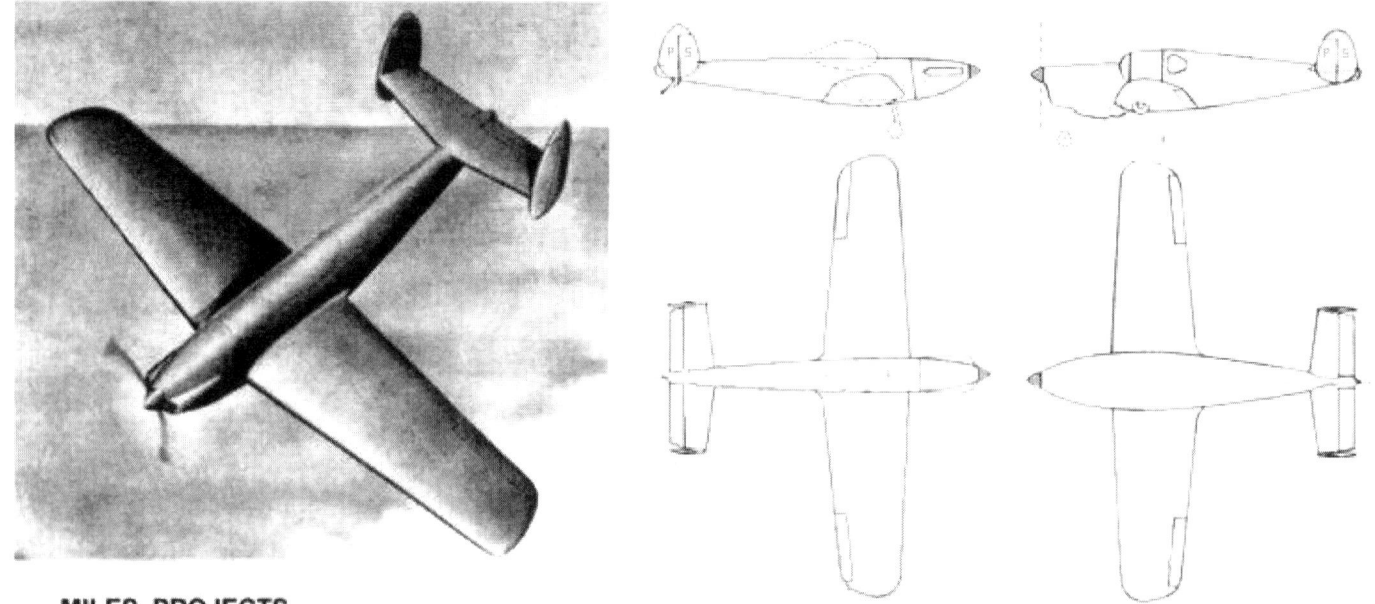

MILES PROJECTS

M. 47 - A design proposal for a radio controlled target aircraft,
Using the wings and tailplane of the M.28 and using a cheap and readily available engine of 220 h.p. at 12,000 ft.
M. 47 A - The 250 h.p. De Havilland Gipsy Queen engine was to be used temporarily until the cheaper engine became available.
Not developed.
Performance
Maximum speed at 12,000 ft. 230 m.p.h. - 225 m.p.h. A.
Climb rate to 12,000 ft. 6 mins. - 7 mins. A.
Duration. 4 hrs.
Dimensions - Span. 30 ft. 6 ins. - Length. 24 ft. - 24 ft. 6 ins. A - Wing area. 160 sq. ft.
Weights - Empty. 1,230 lbs. - Loaded. 1,870 lbs.

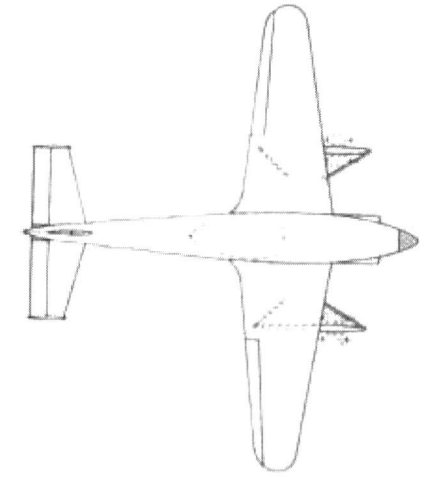

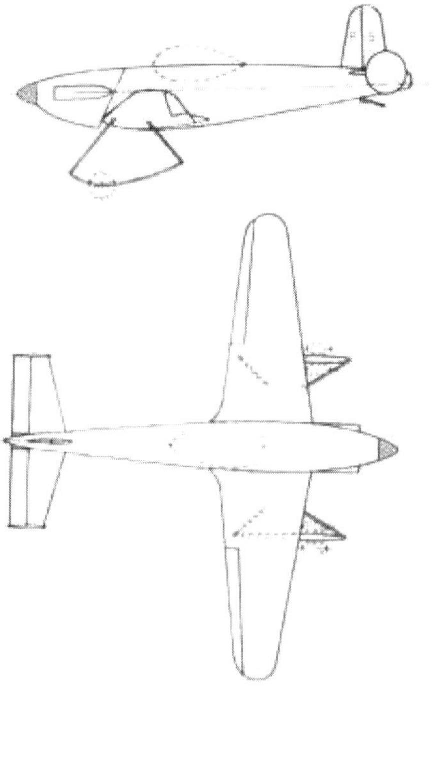

M. 49 - Similar to the M. 47 but smaller.
Fitted with jettisonable wheels on take off and skids for landing.
Not developed.
Performance
Maximum speed at 12,000 ft. 320 m.p.h.
Climb rate to 12,000 ft. 4 mins.
Duration. 4 hrs.
Dimensions
Span. 21 ft. 6 ins. - Length. 19 ft. 6 ins.
Wing area. 70 sq. ft.
Weights
Empty. 900 lbs. - Loaded. 1,550 lbs.

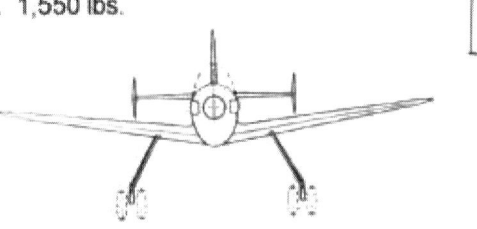

MILES PROJECTS

1943 - M. 51 - 'MINERVA' - A design for a twin engined transport aircraft, with accommodation for eight passenger and a crew of two.
Of an all metal stressed skin construction, fitted with retractable tricycle undercarriage.
Powered by two 295 h.p. De Havilland Gipsy Queen IV engines or if more powerful engines were required two 425 h.p. Armstrong Siddeley Cheetah XV engines.
Not submitted, due to outside influences.

Performance
Cruising speed. 165 m.p.h. D.H. - 190 m.p.h. A.S.
Climb rate. 1,190 ft./min.
Range. 600 miles.
Fuel capacity. 80 gallons.
Oil   "   8   "

Dimensions
Span. 52 ft. - Length. 29 ft.
Wing area. 350 sq. ft.

Weights
Empty. 4,393 lbs.
Loaded. 7,725 lbs. D.H. - 8,450 lbs. A.S.

1943 - M. 53 - Spec. T. 23 / 43. - An elementary side by side two seat training type, with dual controls and an option for a third seat behind the front two.

M. 53 A - Powered by 250 h.p. De Havilland Gipsy Six III engine or 205 h.p. D.H.Gipsy Queen II engine or 295 h.p. D.H.Gipsy Queen IV engine.

Performance
Maximum speed. 123 m.p.h. to 160 m.p.h
Cruising   "   120 m.p.h. to 137 m.p.h.
Climb rate. 840 ft./min. to 1,100 ft./min.
      "   "   to 5,000 ft.
         4 mins. 25 secs. to 6 mins. 55 secs.
Service ceiling. 15,000 ft. to 24,000 ft.

Dimensions
Span. 36 ft. - Length. 27 ft. 9 ins.
Wing area. 213 sq. ft.

Weights
Empty. 2,132 lbs. to 2,261 lbs.
Loaded. 3,047 lbs. to 3,176 lbs.

M. 53 B - Powered by 250 h.p. De Havilland Gipsy Six III engine or 295 h.p. D.H.Gipsy Queen IV engine or 340 h.p. Armstrong Siddeley Cheetah XIX engine.

Performance
Maximum speed. 125 m.p.h. to 161 m.p.h.
Cruising   "   120 m.p.h. to 135 m.p.h.
Climb rate. 959 ft./min. to 1,075 ft./min.
      "   "   to 5,000 ft. 4 mins. 10 secs. to 5 mins. 35 secs.
Service ceiling. 17,000 ft. to 24,000 ft.
Dimensions - Span. 38 ft. - Length. 29 ft. - Wing area. 240 sq. ft.
Weights
Empty. 2,316 lbs. to 2,695 lbs. - Loaded. 3,231 lbs. to 3,610 lbs.

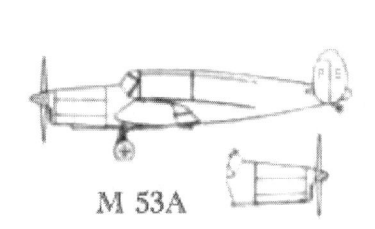

M. 53 C - Powered by 160 h.p. De Havilland Gipsy Major III engine.

Performance
Maximum speed. 130 m.p.h.
Cruising   "   120 m.p.h.
Climb rate. 825 ft./min.
      "   "   to 5,000 ft. 7 mins.
Service ceiling. 15,500 ft.

Dimensions -
Span. 36 ft. - Length. 29 ft.
Wing area. 191 sq. ft.

Weights
Empty. 1,773 lbs. - Loaded. 2,620 lbs.

M. 53 D - As the M. 53 C, but with a single fin & rudder.

M 53A

M 53D

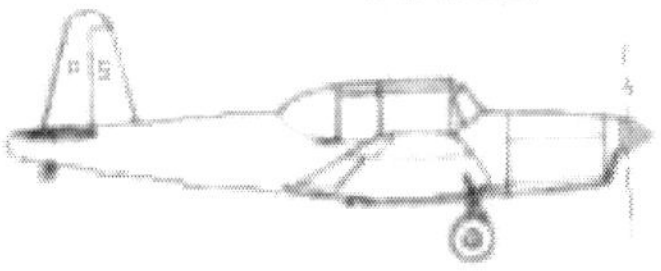

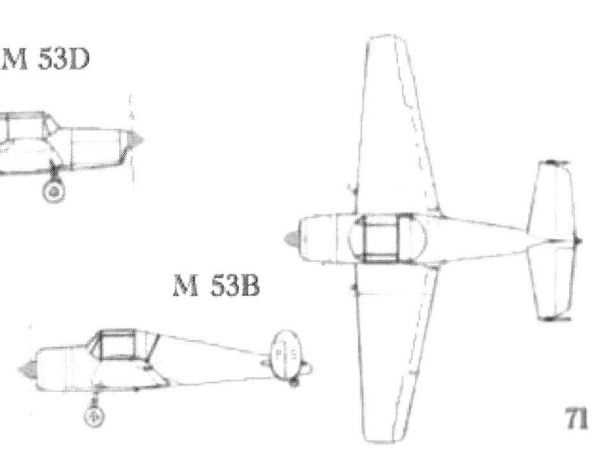

M 53B

MILES PROJECTS

1944 - M. 54 - A design for a twin engined transport type, with accommodation for seventeen passengers. Of an all metal stressed skin construction.
Powered by two 1,090 h.p. Bristol Taurus VI engines.

Performance
Cruising speed at 6,000 ft. 210 m.p.h.
Climb rate. 1,650 ft./min.
Range. 1,650 miles.

Dimensions
Span. 64 ft.
Length. 49 ft.
Wing area. 500 sq. ft.

Weights
Empty. 10,090 lbs.
Loaded. 16,580 lbs.

M. 54 A - As M. 54, but with tricycle undercarriage and with accommodation for twenty passengers.
Powered by two 1,010 h.p. Bristol Perseus XX engines.
Dimensions - Span. 64 ft. - Length. 50 ft. - Wing area. 520 sq. ft.
Weights - Empty. 11,500 lbs. - Loaded. 20,000 lbs.

1944 - M. 55 - 'MARLBOROUGH' - A design for a four engined multi-purpose aircrew training aircraft. To be built from as many standard parts as possible.
Powered by four 730 h.p. Bristol Mercury XXV engines.
As an aircrew trainer fitted with two gun turrets, one in the nose and the other in the tail.
" for flying training without the turrets.
" a twenty paratroop version plus their equipment, there were to be doors amidships on the port and starboard sides of the fuselage, plus another in the floor.
As a mine layer with two tons of mines and a crew of three.
The front turret was removed, the rear turret having four Browning machine guns.
As an unarmed ambulance, twelve stretcher cases could be carried with a crew of five.
A transport type it could carry two and half tons of military equipment.
As a glider tug it could tow a Horsa glider loaded with 16,000 lbs. of equipment.
Not developed.

Performance
Maximum speed at 16,000 ft. 286 m.p.h.
Cruising speed. 150 m.p.h. eco.
Range. 1,350 miles.
Duration. 10 hrs. maximum.

Dimensions
Span. 77 ft.
Length. 64 ft.
Wing area. 737 sq. ft.

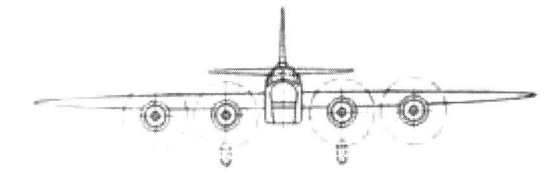

Weights - Empty. 15,690 lbs.
As a bomber, mine laying or freighter- Loaded. 27,750 lbs.
" " glider tug trainer   -   "   22,800 lbs
" an aircrew trainer or ambulance - "   25,000 lbs.
" for paratroop training   -   "   27,100 lbs.
" " flying training   -   "   20,000 lbs.

MILES PROJECTS

M. 56 - A twin engined transport aircraft, with accommodation for twenty four passengers in a pressurised cabin.
Of an all metal stressed skin construction and with tricycle undercarriage.
Powered by two 1,620 h.p. Rolls-Royce Merlin 24 water cooled engines or two Bristol Perseus radial engines.
If a four engined type was required, Armstrong Siddeley engines could have been fitted.

Performance
Maximum speed at 10,000 ft. 310 m.p.h.
Cruising   "   " 7,000 ft. 194 m.p.h.
Climb rate. 1,650 ft./min.
   "   "   to 10,000 ft. 6 mins.
Range. 1,600 miles max.
Fuel capacity. 815 gallons.
Oil   "   60   "

Dimensions
Span. 80 ft. - Length. 66 ft.
Wing area. 800 sq. ft.

Weights
Empty. 13,340 lbs. - Loaded. 25,600 lbs.

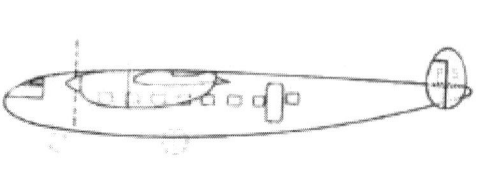

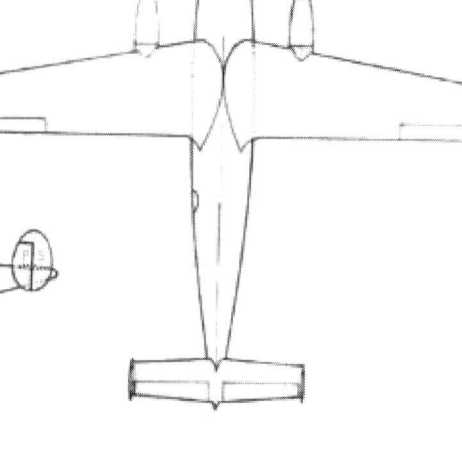

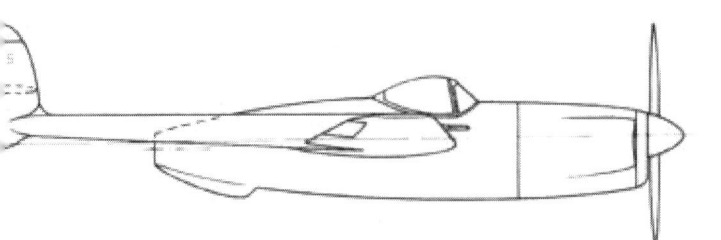

M. 58 - A Naval patrol fighter aircraft.
Powered by a 500 h.p. piston engine and also fitted with a Power Jets W.2/700 engine.
The ability to have a long duration and range on the piston engine, whilst having speed of the jet engine in attack.
Armed with two forward firing Hispano Suiza cannon, mounted in the forward ends of the tail boom.
Not developed.

Performance
Maximum speed at 27,000 ft. 463 m.p.h.
Duration. 7 hrs.

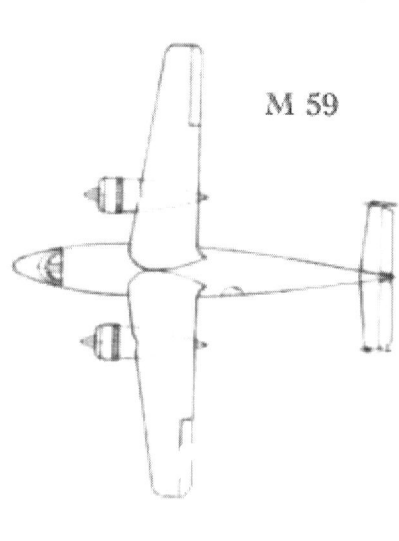

MILES PROJECTS

M. 59 - A design similar to the M. 54 project.
A twin engined civil transport aircraft, with a crew of two and accommodation for thirteen passengers.
Of an all metal construction.
Powered by two 585 h.p. Armstrong Siddeley engines.

M. 59 A - *Spec. NR / A. 15* - A version of the M.59 as a communications type, for the Navy.
Powered by two 500 h.p. Alvis Leonides engines.

M. 59 B - Powered by two 340 h.p. Armstrong Siddeley Cheetah X engines.

Performance
Cruising speed. 190 m.p.h. - 204 m.p.h. A - 160 m.p.h. B.
Climb rate. 930 ft./min. A - 940 ft./min. B.
" " on one engine. 270 ft./min. A - 200 ft./min.
Range. 1,000 miles. - 920 miles. A - 800 miles. B.

Dimensions
Span. 57 ft. - 55 ft. A / B.
Length. 50 ft. - 46 ft. 1 ins. A / B.
Wing area. 400 sq. ft.

Weights
Empty. 7,400 lbs. - 8,125 lbs. A - 8,100 lbs. B.
Loaded. 12,000 lbs. - 12,670 lbs. A - 11,270 lbs. B.

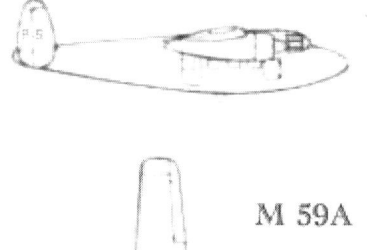

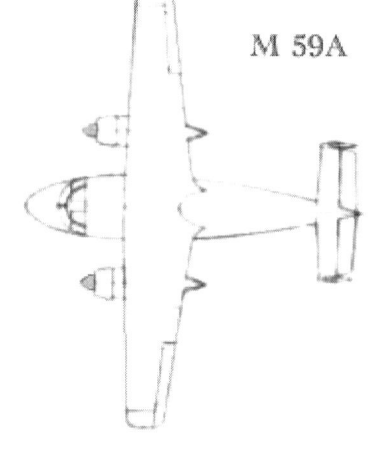

M 59

M 59A

M. 61 - A design for a single engined Military freighter type, with similarities to the Aerovan.
Of an all wooden construction, other than the metal tail boom.
Powered by a 1,600 h.p. Wright Cyclone GR-2600 A5B two row radial engine or a Bristol Hercules engine.
Not developed.

Performance
Cruising speed. 165 m.p.h.
Range. 1,100 miles.

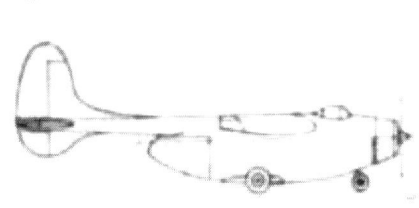

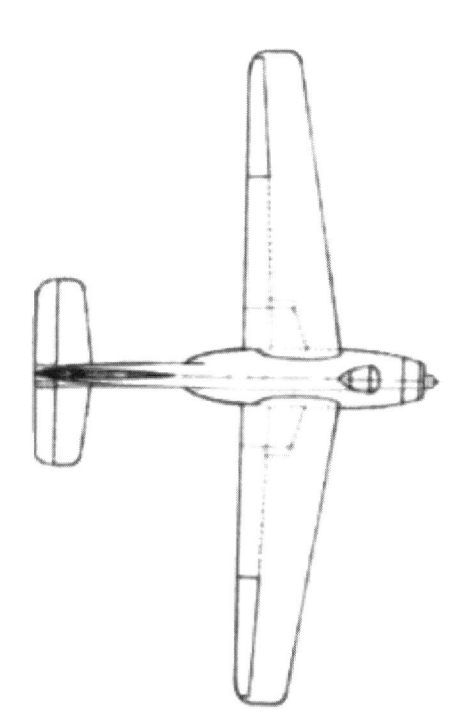

Dimensions
Span. 94 ft. - Length. 58 ft. 6 ins.
Wing area. 1,100 sq. ft.

Weights
Empty. 11,290 lbs. - Loaded. 24,000 lbs.

MILES PROJECTS

M. 62 - A design similar to the M.61, but larger.
Of an all metal construction, with loading doors and each end of the fuselage.
Powered by two 1,600 h.p. Wright Cyclone GR-2600 A5B engines or Bristol Hercules engines.
Able carry a load of seven and a half tons in a hold thirty feet long.
Not developed.
Performance - Cruising speed. 170 m.p.h. - Range. 1,100 miles.
Dimensions - Span. 110 ft. - Length. 69 ft. - Wing area. 1,500 sq. ft.
Weights - Empty. 20,960 lbs. - Loaded. 45,120 lbs.

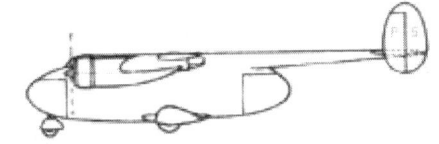

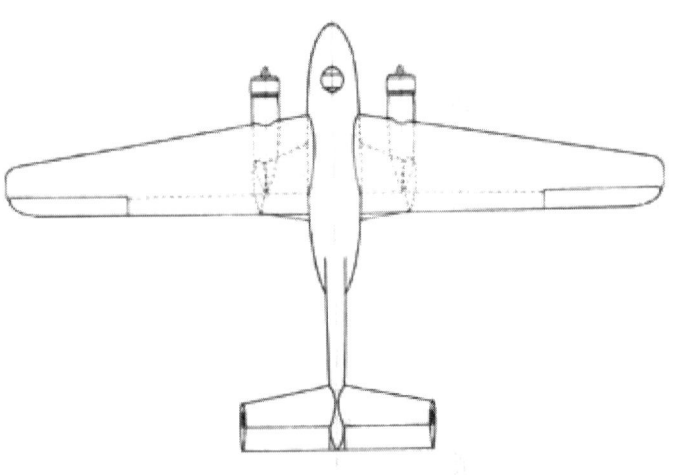

M. 63 - A Libellula designed Maiplane
Powered by three Power Jets W.2/700 engines or three Rolls-Royce B 37 engines.
Not developed.
Performance
Cruising speed at 36,000 ft. 500 m.p.h.
Range. 1,000 miles.
Fuel capacity. 585 gallons.
Dimensions
Span. 39 ft. 3 ins. front - 55 ft. rear.
Length. 35 ft. 9 ins.
Wing area. 139 sq. ft. front - 417 sq. ft. rear.
Weights
Empty. 12,875 lbs. - Loaded. 22,500 lbs.

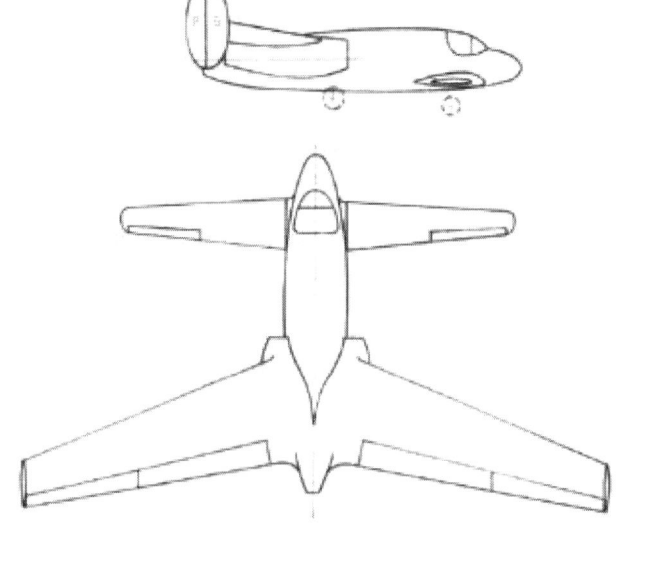

MILES PROJECTS

M. 66 - *Spec. A. 4 / 45.* - A design for a three seat communications aircraft, for the Army.
Powered by 250 h.p. De Havilland Gipsy Queen 31 engine and fitted with a retractable undercarriage.
Performance
Cruising speed. 100 m.p.h. - Landing speed. 30 m.p.h. - Climb rate. 500 ft./min.
Service ceiling. 10,000 ft. - Duration. 2 hrs. 30 mins.

M. 67 - A design for a four engined transport aircraft, with accommodation for 20 to 32 passengers and underfloor luggage compartments.
Of an all metal construction and fitted with a tricycle undercarriage.
Powered by four Rolls-Royce Dart turboprop engines.
Not required.
Performance
Cruising speed at 10,000 ft. 275 to 300 m.p.h. - Climb rate. 1,750 ft./min. - Range. 1,050 miles.
Dimensions - Span. 80 ft. - Length. 66 ft. - Wing area. 800 sq. ft.
Weights - Empty. 16,050 lbs. - Loaded. 30,000 lbs.

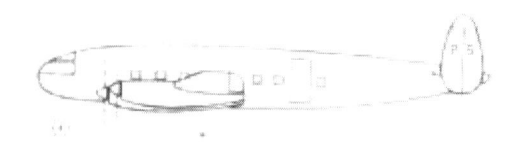

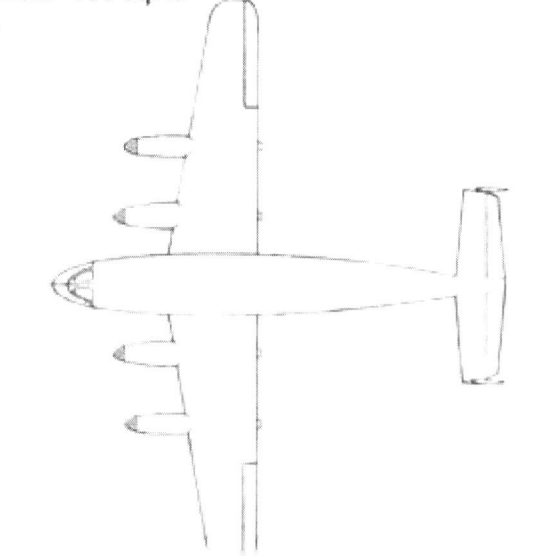

MILES PROJECTS

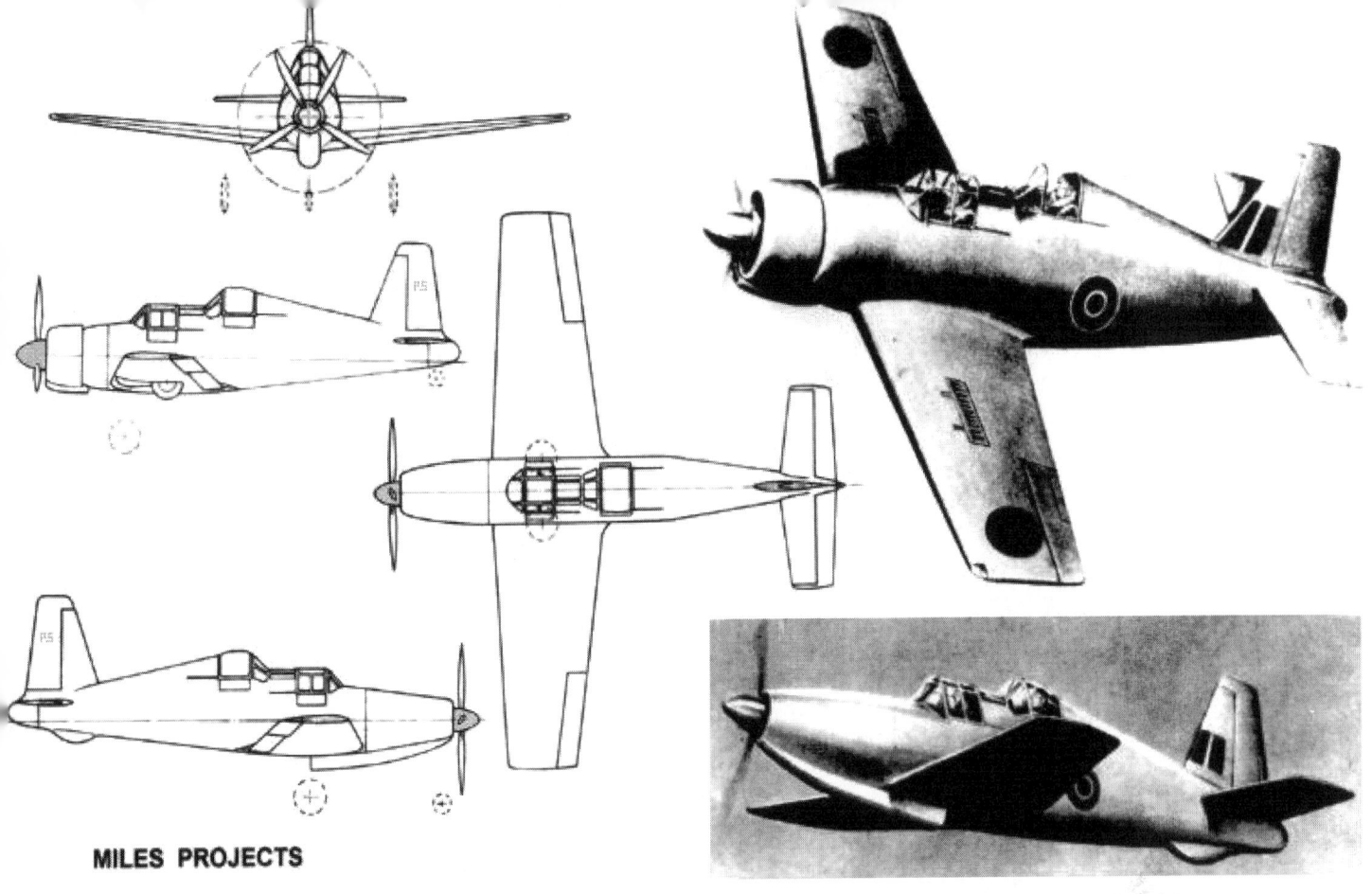

1946 - M. 70 - *Spec. T. 7/45* - A design for a two seat advanced trainer, for flying, gunnery and bombing purposes.
Powered by 500 h.p. Alvis Leonides or 500 h.p. Napier E.127 or 500 h.p Bristol turboprop engines.
Fitted with tricycle or normal undercarriage, plus dive brakes in the wings.
The instructor sat in the rear cockpit, on a raised seat with a good all round view.

Performance
Maximum speed. 245 m.p.h. Alvis - 248 m.p.h. Napier - 262 m.p.h. Bristol.
Cruising   " 235 m.p.h.   " - 220 m.p.h.   "   - 230 m.p.h.   "
Climb rate. 1,600 ft./min. Alvis - 2,330 ft./min. Napier - 2,550 ft./min. Bristol.
    "   " to 5,000 ft. 3 mins. 5 secs. Alvis - 2 mins. 20 secs. Napier / Bristol.
Fuel capacity. 50 gallons.
Oil   "   5   "

Dimensions
Span. 31 ft. 4 ins. - Length. 26 ft. 2 ins.
Wing area. 172 sq. ft.

Weights
Empty. 2,823 lbs. Alvis.
Loaded. 4,150 lbs.   "

M. 72 - A project similar to the M. 71 Merchantman.

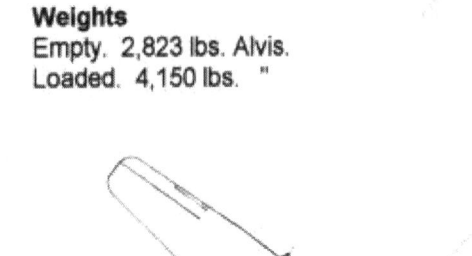

M. 73 - A design similar to the Marathon but larger, for a four engined high wing transport aircraft.

MILES PROJECTS

1947 - M. 74 - A design for a two seater aircraft using many Messenger parts, during 1947. Powered by a 100 h.p. Blackburn Cirrus Minor II engine.   -   Not produced.
Performance
Maximum speed. 116 m.p.h.
Cruising   "   100 m.p.h.
Climb rate. 700 ft./min.
Service ceiling. 13,000 ft.
Range. 400 miles.
Fuel capacity. 18 gallons.
Oil   "   2 1/2 "
Dimensions
Span. 36 ft. 2 ins. - Length. 34 ft.
Height. 6 ft. 2 ins. - Wing area. 191 sq. ft.
Weights
Empty. 1,190 lbs. - Loaded. 1,687 lbs.

M. 101 - *later renumbered* > **M. 102** - A project for a large four engine car transport aircraft, for Silver City Airways.
Accommodation for thirty two passengers and able to carry six cars.
Powered by four Rolls-Royce Dart turboprop engines.
Not developed.

M. 103 - A project using the Hurel-Dubois high lift wing, for a three ton military freighter.
Powered by two 500 h.p. Alvis Leonides engines and a 1,800 lb.s.t. Rolls-Royce Soar booster engine, for take off.
Dimensions - Span. 150 ft.

M. 104 - Similar to M. 103 but larger, also using the Hurel-Dubios wing and as a military freighter of six ton.
Powered by two 870 h.p. Alvis Leonides Majors engines, plus two 1,800 lb.s.t. Rolls-Royce Soar booster engines.
Dimensions - Span. 148 ft. 7 ins. - Wing area. 1,076 sq. ft.

M. 109 - A project using a semi-Hurel-Dubios wing, for a six seat utility aircraft.
Powered by two 150 h.p. Lycoming O-320 engines.

1959 - M. 110 - Various research studies, into delta wing designs.
A - A glider type, towed underneath a helicopter.
Dimensions - Span. 15 ft. - Length. 20 ft.
B - Similar to A, but more complex and heavier, either as a glider or jet powered.
Dimensions - Span. 20 ft. - Length. 40 ft.

M. 111 - A projected utility type with six seats, powered by a 320 h.p. Turbomeca Astazou engine.

Not allocated - Three projects - A - For a high speed tail first type.
B - Similar to the D.H.Chipmunk, as a A.O.P. type.
C - An A.O.P. type, with deflected thrust and S.T.O.L. capabilities, powered by Armstrong Siddeley Viper engine.

M. 112 - Project for a twin engined five seat executive type, powered by two 250 h.p. Allison engines.

M. 113 - A project for an Army aircraft, in collaboration with Auster.

MILES PROJECTS

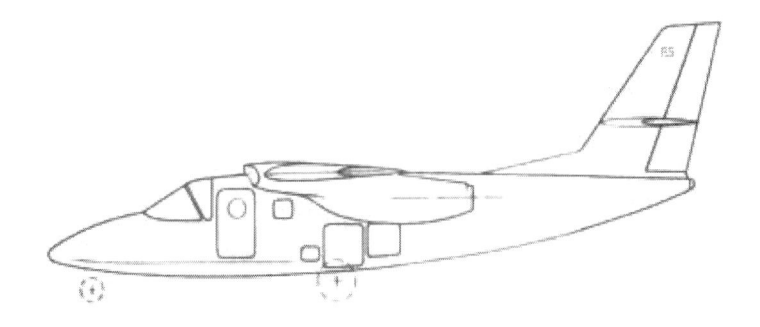

1963 - MILES CENTURY - A projected 7 / 8 seater executive jet aircraft, similar to the M.100, but larger.
Of an all metal stressed skin construction, on a retractable tricycle undercarriage.
Powered by two 1,540 lb.s.t. Turbomeca Aubisque engines.
A mock up was built and a design was submitted during 1964.
A grant was allowed for half of the costs to manufacture the aircraft - £ 400,000 =
The other half of it was to be raised by Miles, which they were unable to do.
Not produced, but would have sold at around £ 80,000 =

Performance
Maximum speed. 452 m.p.h.
Cruising   "   350 m.p.h. eco.
Climb rate. 3,100 ft./min. - 1,050 ft./min. on 1.
Service ceiling. 14,000 ft.
Range. 1,600 miles.

Dimensions
Span. 40 ft. - Length. 41 ft. 6 ins.
Height. 14 ft. - Wing area. 270 sq. ft.

Weights
Empty. 4,760 lbs. - Loaded. 10,000 lbs.

ROLLS-ROYCE DART

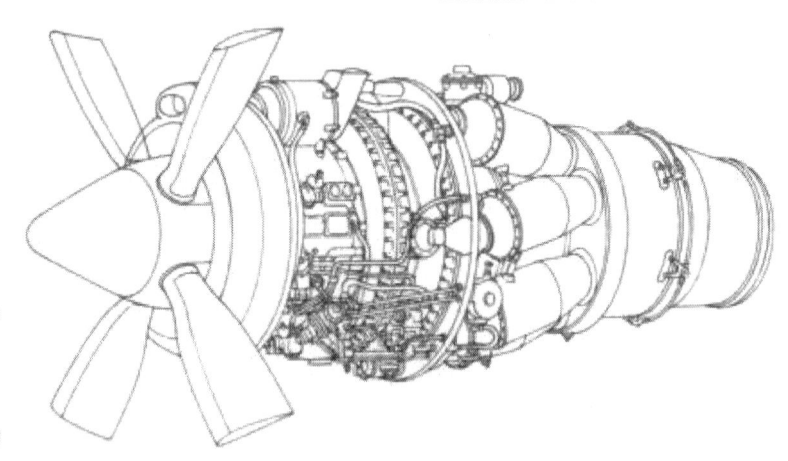

Right and below The Rolls-Royce Dart, which made its first bench run in 1946, was the earliest turboprop to go into service. The Dart remains in production after more than 30 years, and over 7,000 have been delivered

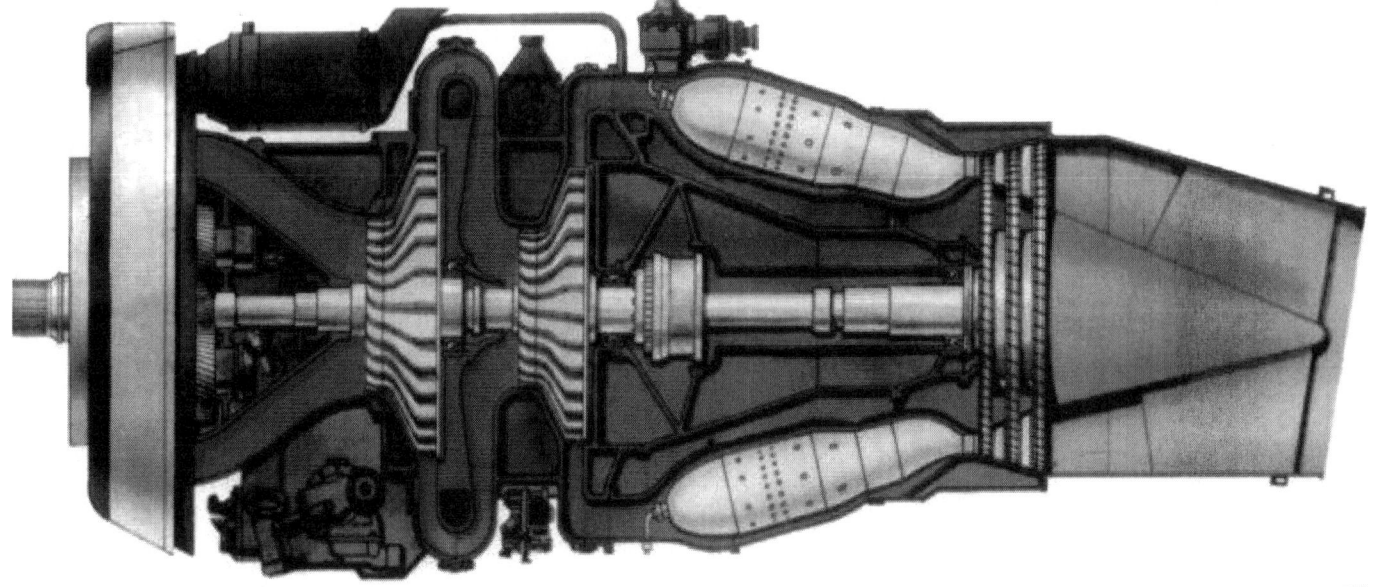

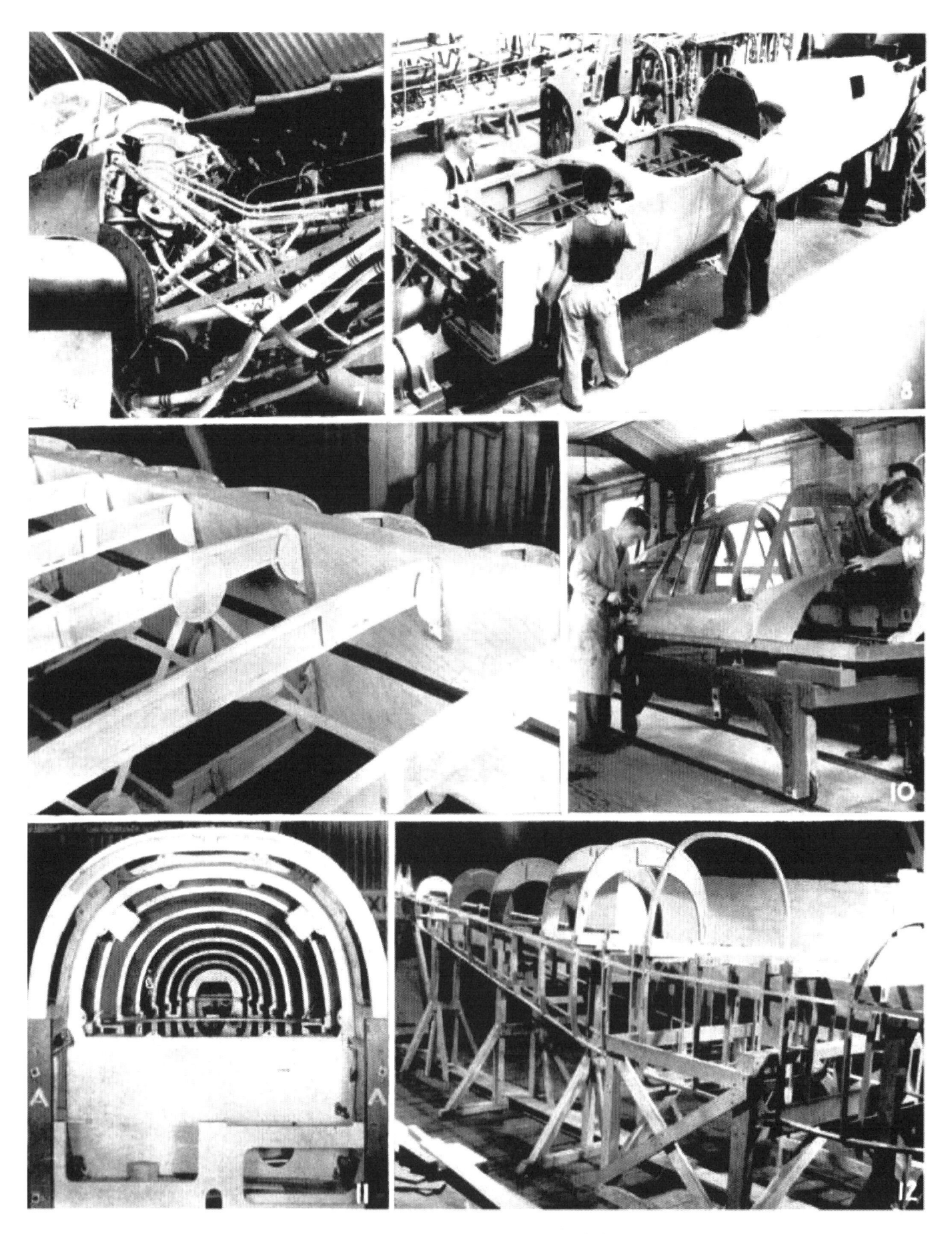

MILES CONSTRUCTIONAL METHODS

7. Junction of wing root, front fuselage and engine mounting of a Master. 8. Master fuselage after the skin has been applied. 9. Wing rib attachments to a front spar. 10. Master cabin-top assembly. 11. Looking aft through the Mercury M.28 fuselage. 12. A typical light fuselage framework assembly.

MILES Aircraft Ltd.

	PAGE
Miles Aircraft	1
" " Construction methods	2
Martlet - Hornet Baby - Southern Martlet - Gnat Biplane	3
Metal Martlet	4
M I Satyr	5
M 2 Hawk - IIA - IIB - IIC - IID	6
" " Major - IIF - IIE / Gipsy Six Hawk / Hawk Speed Six - IIG / H / L / M / P / R / S / T	7
" " " - IIU / W / X / Y	8
M 3 Falcon - IIIA Falcon Major - IIIB / C / D / E - Gillette Falcon	9
M 4 Merlin	10
M 5 Sparrowhawk - M VA	11
M 6 Hawcon	12
M 7 Nighthawk - M VIIA	13
M 8 Peregrine	14
M 9 Kestrel	15
M 9 A Master I / IA - M 19 Master II	16
Master - *Skeleton*	17
M 24 Master Fighter - M 27 Master III	18
Master - *pictures & plan*	19
M 11 Whitney Straight - IIA / B / C	20
M 12 Mohawk	21
M 13 Hobby	22
M 14 Magister - 14A Hawk Trainer Mk.III - 14B Hawk Trainer Mk.II	23
" " - Numbers	24
" " - *skeleton & cockpit*	25
" " - Numbers	26
" " - *pictures & plan*	27
M 15	28
M 16 Mentor	29
M 17 Monarch	30
M 18 - I / II / III - HL	31
M 20	32
M 25 Martinet - TT I - M 50 Queen Martinet	33
Martinet - Queen Martinet	34
M 28 - I / II / III / IV / V / VI	35
M 30 X Minor	36
M 33 Monitor - TT I / II	37
M 35	38
M 37	39
M 38 Messenger - I - II A / B / C - III - IV / B - V	40
M 38 " III - M 48 Messenger	41
M 39B Libellula	42
M 52	43
M 57 Aerovan - I - II - III - IV - V - VI - M 57A - M 72	44
" " - *specs, pictures & plan*	45
M 60 Marathon - M 69 Marathon II	46
M 64 - LR 5	47
M 65 Gemini - IA - IA Special - IB - II / A - III / A / B / C - IV - VII - VIII	48
" " - Numbers - *cockpit & plan*	49
M 68 Boxcar	50
M 71 Merchantman	51
M 75 Aries	52
M 76 - M 77 Sparrowjet - M 78 to M 99	53
M 100 Student - II - IV / V Centurion	54
H.D.M. 105 - 106 Caravan - 107 Aerojeep - 108	55
M 114 - I / II / M 117 - M 115 / 218	56
MILES Projects	57 to 79
1933 - 1935 M 10 - 1936 - 1940 - M 21 / 36 / 55	57
M 22 / A	58
M 23 / A	59

	Page
MILES AIRCRAFT	
Projects	
1942	60
M 26 X Projects - X 2 - X 3 - X 4 - X 5 - X 6 - X 7 - X 8	61
X 9 - X 10	62
X 11 - X 12 - X 13	63
X 14 - X 15	64
M 29 - M 31 - M 32	65
M 34 - M 36	66
M 39 - M 40	67
M 41 - M 42 - M 43 - M 44	68
M 45 - M 46	69
M 47 / A - M 49	70
M 51 Minerva - M 53 / A / B / C / D	71
M 54 / A - M 55 Marlborough	72
M 56 - M 58	73
MM 59 / A / B - M 61	74
M 62 - M 63	75
M 66 - M 67	76
M 70 - M 72 - M 73	77
M 74 - M 101 - M 102 - M 103 - M 104 - M 109 - M 110 - M 111 - M 112 - M 113	78
1963 Miles Century - *Rolls-Royce Dart*	79
Miles construction methods.	80

H.M.S. BULWARK.
Built by Harland & Wolff Ltd. at Belfast.
Laid down. 10-5-1945.   -   Launched. 22-6-1948.   -   Completed. 4-11-1954.
Displacement. 22,000 tons. - Loaded. 27,000 tons.
Length. 737 ft. 9 ins.   -   Beam. 123 ft.   -   Speed. 28 knots.   -   Cost. £ 10,386,000.=
With a five and half degree angled deck, two hydraulic catapults, two central deck lifts and mirror landing aid.
Later converted to a commando carrier, with helicopters and fully convertible to anti-submarine role.
Powered by 78,000 hp. Parsons geared turbines. - two shafts.
Armed with twenty 40 mm. anti-aircraft guns and four 3 pounders.
A complement of up to 1,390 crew members and up to 45 aircraft can be carried.

ORDER YOUR COPY HERE NOW

KITES, BIRDS & STUFF.

MANUFACTURERS AIRCRAFT of GREAT BRITAIN

A series of seventeen books on various manufactures - these apply to the larger groups.

ARMSTRONG WHITWORTH Aircraft	AVRO Aircraft
BLACKBURN Aircraft	BOULTON PAUL Aircraft
BRISTOL Aircraft	De HAVILLAND Aircraft
FAIREY Aircraft	GLOSTER Aircraft
HANDLEY PAGE Aircraft	HAWKER Aircraft
MILES Aircraft	The ROYAL AIRCRAFT FACTORY + INFLATABLES
SHORT Aircraft	SOPWITH Aircraft
SUPERMARINE Aircraft	VICKERS Aircraft
WESTLAND Aircraft.	

KITES, BIRDS & STUFF
Over 150 Years of BRITISH Aviation
Makers & Manufacturers

Vol. 1 - A to C   -   Vol. 2 - D to O   -   Vol. 3 - P to Z

A series of three volumes.
Each volume contains around 260 pages with details of various manufacturers aircraft.
Omitted from the Manufactures series of books. :- *goto website for more details.*

Enjoy.

Available at a Later Date :-

KITES, BIRDS & STUFF - Aircraft of GERMANY.

KITES, BIRDS & STUFF - Aircraft of the UNITED STATES of AMERICA.

KITES, BIRDS & STUFF -
     Aircraft of the UNION of the SOVIET SOCIALISTS REPUBLIC (*RUSSIA*)

A small note from the Author :-

I do hope you enjoy this book as I felt that all the information that it holds would eventually be lost or forgotten.
The trials and tribulations of others in times of peace and war should be remembered, for if not now but for future generations.
Less we forget.
It has taken me a number of years to put these works together.
It may have all started back in the 1940's or 1950's.
My growing years were shaped around Hornchurch Aerodrome, which must have by some means affected me one way or another ?
If you read the Horchurch Aerodrome section of :-
Kites, Birds & Stuff - Volume 2 - D to O - this may give you an insight.
At Suttons School during the early 1950's, I began to put these projects together.
It was put on hold for reasons of - life, work, money, family, marriage, children - all the main reasons why we exist.
Eventually the time was right, after I had retired and that we now had computers.
I downloaded all my information, which I had saved and more.
I collated everything and eventually I produced my series of books, for myself.
By chance a friend who was visiting saw my work and told me in no uncertain terms :-
'That I should get it published and out there for people to see'.
I have done just that.
There may be more to come (*Big 'G' willing*) only time will tell, as I work alone.
Either way I do hope you enjoy what is available.

P.D.Stemp

Printed in Great Britain
by Amazon.co.uk, Ltd.,
Marston Gate.